'This book is a must-read for police practitioners, academics, professional policing students, and policing scholars. At a time when gender-responsive policing and security are gaining traction domestically and internationally, Emma Cunningham fills a void within the contemporary literature on women in policing, drawing upon contemporary research and using original data to shed light upon gender inequality, sexism, and misogyny in the everyday lives of female police officers in the UK and beyond. This book will serve as a wake-up call for policymakers, police leaders, and trainers'.

Dr Wendy Laverick, *Programme Director Professional Policing, Hull University*

'This book is a clear-sighted exploration of twenty-first-century policing and its impact on women. Emma Cunningham holds current events and practices up to the light of diverse historical sources, in a call to action that is urgent and constructive. She tackles the myth of women's "nature" via Mary Wollstonecraft's pioneering arguments on Justice and human rights, and in doing so delivers a powerful case for an intersectional approach to policing.

Cunningham was a long-term supporter of the Wollstonecraft memorial artwork, well before the controversy kicked in. Like that memorial, this book ensures that Wollstonecraft is, in Virginia Woolf's words, "alive and active […] even now among the living".

With this feminist critique of police work in Britain and beyond, Cunningham draws on Wollstonecraft's key principles and takes them into action, which is exactly where they belong. I learnt a lot from this book and I am filled with hope that others will learn too'.

Bee Rowlatt, *journalist, writer and activist.*
She chaired the Mary on the Green campaign to memorialise Mary Wollstonecraft and is a founding Trustee of the human rights education charity the Wollstonecraft Society

Women in Policing

Women in Policing provides an insight into women's role within policing, their emergence, and development, offering a theoretical underpinning to explore this role as well as incorporating two empirical studies, one which reassesses the lived experiences of female officers, and one based on FOI requests to examine police officer disciplinary offences in three police force areas.

The book begins by exploring some of the history of ideas in relation to ideas about women and their supposed nature. Cunningham shows how a variety of feminist ideas and critique are of vital importance in illuminating and critiquing the place of women within this field and provides a feminist lens with which to explore these themes critically. The book also examines the re-emergence of these ideas about women in current women and policing literature. Together, exploration of these sources using a feminist conceptual framework facilitates a new, rich analysis that is both reflective and reflexive, culminating in a novel snapshot of the place of women in policing in England. She argues that accepting both institutional racism and institutional misogyny are vital in approaching transformational change in policing practice. The book concludes with a discussion around how these findings can help with police confidence and legitimacy in the future.

A fundamental examination of the ideas underpinning how women's integration and continuation in policing has happened, where it is currently, and where it may go, *Women in Policing* will be of great interest to police practitioners and students as well as Criminology, Sociology, and Law and Policing scholars.

Emma Cunningham is a senior lecturer in Criminology at the University of East London. She has worked within different departments in higher education for over 20 years and has taught undergraduate and post-graduate students across the social sciences as well as local, national, and international police officers. She was also involved in the England–Africa Partnership between staff at the University of Teesside, from the Kigali Institute of Education, the National University of Rwanda, and the Rwandan Police, and was an external examiner there (2007–08). She is interested in Wollstonecraft, feminism, domestic and sexual violence, citizenship, human rights, and women and policing, which inform her research areas.

Routledge Frontiers of Criminal Justice

Emotional Labour in Criminal Justice and Criminology
Edited by Jake Phillips, Chalen Westaby, Andrew Fowler and Jaime Waters

Predictive Policing and Artificial Intelligence
Edited by John L. M. McDaniel and Ken G. Pease

The Use of Victim Impact Statements in Sentencing for Sexual Offences
Stories of Strength
Rhiannon Davies and Lorana Bartels

Understanding the Educational Experiences of Imprisoned Men
(Re)education
Helen Nichols

Professionalism in Probation
Making Sense of Marketisation
Matt Tidmarsh

Policing Child Sexual Abuse
Failure, Corruption and Reform in Queensland
Paul Bleakley

Collaboration and Innovation in Criminal Justice
An Activity Theory Alternative to Offender Rehabilitation
Paulo Rocha

For more information about this series, please visit: www.routledge.com/Routledge-Frontiers-of-Criminal-Justice/book-series/RFCJ

Women in Policing
Feminist Perspectives on
Theory and Practice

Emma Cunningham

LONDON AND NEW YORK

First published 2022
by Routledge
2 Park Square, Milton Park, Abingdon, Oxon OX14 4RN

and by Routledge
605 Third Avenue, New York, NY 10158

Routledge is an imprint of the Taylor & Francis Group, an informa business

© 2022 Emma Cunningham

The right of Emma Cunningham to be identified as author of this work
has been asserted by her in accordance with sections 77 and 78 of the
Copyright, Designs and Patents Act 1988.

All rights reserved. No part of this book may be reprinted or reproduced or utilised
in any form or by any electronic, mechanical, or other means, now known or
hereafter invented, including photocopying and recording, or in any information
storage or retrieval system, without permission in writing from the publishers.

Trademark notice: Product or corporate names may be trademarks or registered trademarks,
and are used only for identification and explanation without intent to infringe.

British Library Cataloguing-in-Publication Data
A catalogue record for this book is available from the British Library

Library of Congress Cataloging-in-Publication Data
A catalog record has been requested for this book

ISBN: 978-0-367-70182-6 (hbk)
ISBN: 978-0-367-71069-9 (pbk)
ISBN: 978-1-003-14915-6 (ebk)

DOI: 10.4324/9781003149156

Typeset in Times New Roman
by Newgen Publishing UK

This book is dedicated to my lovely family and friends, and to all women and girls

'Rousseau asserts himself that all was right originally: a crowd of authors that all is now right: and I, that all will be right'. (Wollstonecraft, 1792/1994: 79)

Contents

List of tables		x
Acknowledgements		xii
	Introduction: Women in policing – Their sameness and difference	1
1	Wollstonecraft, the 'nature of woman', and women entering the police	8
2	Re-emerging arguments about the nature of woman, a re-examination of twenty-three policewomen data and a review of policing in Australia	27
3	Feminist use of Freedom of Information requests (FOI)	49
4	Conclusions and summary	86
	Bibliography	94
	Index	103

Tables

Service

3.1	Police officers facing disciplinary action by gender 2006–12	56
3.2	Nature of breaches by gender 2006–08	57
3.3	Results of allegations of formal misconduct by Service Police (females; 2006–08)	58
3.4	Results of allegations of formal misconduct by Service Police (males; 2006–08)	59
3.5	Results of formal action by Service Police (females; 2009–11)	60
3.6	Results of formal action by Service Police (males; 2009–11)	61
3.7	Misconduct and formal action: proportions by breach and by gender (2006–11)	62
3.8	Formal action results and breaches female 2011–12	64
3.9	Formal action results and breaches male 2011–12	64

Constabulary

3.1	Alleged offences, type, male and female 2007–11	65
3.2	Rank, offence, verdict and action 2007–11	66
3.3	All serving officers disciplined, breach, and male and female 2011–12	71

Force

3.1	Breach type, male and female officers 2007–12	71
3.2	Breach type, male and female 2011–12	74
3.3	Cases upheld, breach, male and female	75

List of tables xi

3.4	Cases upheld, breach, male and female 2010–11	76
3.5	Cases upheld, breach, male and female 2009–10	76
3.6	Cases upheld, breach, male and female 2008–09	77
3.7	Cases upheld, breach, male and female 2007–08	78

Acknowledgements

Massive thanks are due to everyone who has helped me get this book from the initial ideas to the final draft and the written page. I would like to firstly thank Lydia De Cruz, Commissioning Editor, for supporting me from the concept stage to the short Routledge book fruition, and for taking a risk with me. Many thanks also to Arunima Aditya for keeping me on track and answering all my questions. Special thanks to Dr Wendy Laverick and Bee Rowlatt as well as Jess and Jack for reading and commenting on the early proposals and providing me and the publisher with feedback. Special thanks to Dr Alison Jarvis for the help you gave me with the tables in Chapter 3. You are a star! Many thanks to Bee Rowlatt and Dr Wendy Laverick for also reading the first draft and feeling able to provide an endorsement of this work. I really appreciate this.

My mam, Valerie the matriarch, gets special thanks as she typed up my first undergraduate dissertation on Wollstonecraft 25 years ago, and has always supported and believed in her children. Special thanks to my lovely husband, John, for putting up with me while I have been writing this and who continues to find great red wines and plays Northern for me on a Friday night. My thanks also go always to my children, Jack and Jess, who have grown up with Wollstonecraft, who I am so proud of and who still read, comment, and provide support for everything I do. Jessica's partner Chris, is a fabulous new member of the family, along with Lewis, my stepson, who I am also proud of, who keeps my feet on the ground and makes me laugh, a lot. To Sally, my sister and partner in crime, you keep me going and laughing, and to Anth and Di and Moi and Eric for their support too.

Many thanks to colleagues at Teesside University, John Carter and Alison Jarvis, best curry mates and roomies ever, as well as Craig Ancrum and Margaret Hems at Teesside University. They are all knowledgeable colleagues, academics, and proper friends who are all really

Acknowledgements xiii

good fun and incredibly collegial in challenging times within H.E. To all colleagues at The Junction Foundation who work so hard for the young people in our local community and who are a great team to work with.

To the girls, my closest friends, those who have passed, Liz and Dodi; and those still with me, Fran, Tracey, Polly, Mary, and Cath. We have different views on many things but have stuck together for 30+ years now, so thanks for everything girls.

Bee and Amy, thanks for the personal support and network. It means a lot. You are doing so many great things for women in the community too, which continues to make me optimistic.

To Helima, Judy, Ailsa, Lisa, and Darren here, and Winnie and Graham in Dubs, Daren, Becky, and Marley in Valencia, and Bobby in Australia, thanks a million for your support too and hope we get to see you all again soon

Love Emma x

Introduction
Women in policing: Their sameness and difference

Introduction

We have witnessed extensive changes within policing and police training in England and Wales in the last couple of decades. Shifting from National Police Training being undertaken at specialist centres to Initial Police Learning and Development Programme (IPLDP), approaches to professionalising the police within the areas where they would eventually serve, meant that police culture would begin to change and that there was also an increased number of women entering policing (BAWP, 2014). I had been involved in this teaching and saw some of the implications of allowing the police to attend local university for training during that era rather than having to leave friends, partners, and family to go away to a police training school. The recent aim within the Policing Vision 2025 of recruiting 20,000 more police constables and the introduction of the Policing Education Qualifications Framework (PEQF) from Jan 2020 (College of Policing), has continued the professionalisation agenda of policing in England and Wales. However, even with the equality agendas from the 1970s onwards and discussion about minimising disadvantage, and with positive action in recruitment and promotion more recently with the Equality Act 2010 (Section 159, Legislation.gov.uk), some of the most stubborn challenges facing policing in England and Wales remain. How these challenges are approached and acknowledged within policing is important.

My research interests include gendered and sexual violence, citizenship and human rights, politics, and women in policing, and I aim to address some of the theoretical and empirical problems across these areas within my work. These areas are all informed by gendered inequalities and driven and perpetuated by notions or conceptions about the so-called 'nature' of woman. This book will explore where these ideas about the nature of woman came from and will include an assessment

DOI: 10.4324/9781003149156-1

2 Introduction

of what these have meant and continue to mean. Women's inclusion, integration, and development within policing will be examined at the same time within this work. Having worked with politics, history of ideas as well as criminology and policing programmes for some years, I have built upon the initial ideas I had in relation to women within policing to inform this work. I acknowledge that many of the ideas from this book and a feminist critique could also be used to explore many other organisations, too, such as higher education and the culture therein; however, this work concentrates on women in the police based on my research. This book seeks to explore arguments about the nature of woman and problems from a history of ideas theoretical perspective, which is then applied to empirical research from women officers and disciplinary records from three police service areas in order to add to the body of knowledge in this field. This interdisciplinary approach will utilise some different and innovative methods in discussing the place of women in policing from past ideas to present practice. The arguments about the 'nature' of woman have helped limit what women have been able to do, and while they have changed and been challenged, they can still be seen to re-emerge at times. I hope the analysis and discussion within this book will drive forward the debate about the implementation of transformational change regarding gender, ethnicity, and police culture and discipline. Change is necessary in order for policing to retain any legitimacy and to remain resonant to the communities it serves. Recently an investigation into the nature, prevalence, drivers, and impact of sex discrimination and sexual harassment in the police in Victoria, Australia, illustrated the centrality of gendered inequality to narratives about police culture:

> Family violence is a highly gendered crime and it is symptomatic of, and directly linked to, gender inequality. This inequality presents itself in pervasive sexual harassment in workplaces, sporting clubs, universities and other public spaces. It is manifest in the persistent gender wage gap, the disproportionate burden women carry for caring responsibilities and the growing number of women and children experiencing homelessness seeking safety from violence. It lingers in our outdated notions of roles that are suitable for women and those that are appropriate for men. It is, in its most extreme form, in the sexual assault and abuse of women and young girls and how we believe and support them.
>
> There were several important motivators for this work, but one of the critical questions for Victoria Police was this: 'How can we effectively respond to family and gendered violence if our

own organisation is not a safe place for women to come to work?' Another was: 'How do we best ensure the health, safety and well-being of the organisation's employees?

(VEOHRC, Phase 3, 2019: iv)

This is not just an issue for Australia. Examining gendered inequality in the wider society and on a global scale and how this fits within the culture of male-dominated organisations such as the police is an important area to continue to research. During the COVID-19 pandemic and lockdown in England and Wales, domestic violence and abuse (DVA) levels with survivors reaching out for help have increased massively, with some calling it an epidemic beneath the pandemic (Kelly, 2021). At the core of such crimes is the question of the 'nature' of woman and ideas about man, views around which have been built up and reinforced throughout Western thought, and that, as was noted within the Australian report mentioned above, still impact directly on the notions of what men and women were and are able to do.

This book will begin by briefly exploring feminisms and feminists, as well as adding a discussion about the methodology employed and epistemology issues at play here. Next, it will explore the development of ideas about women and their supposed 'nature' by providing an overview of the main assertions of this from within the history of ideas in Western philosophy. This contextual overview will incorporate historical ideas which have been used to limit women's employment and advancement in many fields, and will be illustrated by feminist theories and those studies written to examine and challenge them. These outdated notions can still be seen informing ideas about women's and men's roles and abilities, and a discussion about how women were able to have joined the police, negotiated, and challenged these ideas within their policing role will be developed.

These ideas will be explored historically from Mary Wollstonecraft's ideas and her two main texts, *A Vindication of the Rights of Men* and *A Vindication of the Rights of Woman* (1790/1994; 1792/1992). Her works cover equality of the sexes as moral creatures with the capacity to reason, and ideas about ethics and justice which still remain useful and have new relevance in understanding women's issues within patriarchal society and male-dominated institutions such as the police. Outdated conceptions regarding women can still be see to emerge hundreds of years after Wollstonecraft critiqued them, and can also clearly still be seen in women and policing literature too. Ideas from later feminists and feminisms will be of use in exploring the place of women and their challenges, including those from Harding (1987), hooks (2000), and

4 *Introduction*

others specifically within the field of women and policing to explore policing culture and practice. While the ideas about a specific character and nature of woman have been discredited over time, ideas associated with these views can still be seen to be articulated and applied in the case of policewomen. Some have argued recently for instance that the honesty stereotype in relation to policewomen remains current (Barnes, Beaulieu, and Saxton, 2017). Feminisms and feminist criminology still have the ability to highlight women's experiences of policing, while women have faced sexist attitudes, harassment, and discrimination, and have been vital in exploring the ways that women have been able to navigate these within their own journey of policing practice. The works of Brown and Heidensohn (2000) as well as Westmarland (2001), Westmarland and Rowe (2018), and Silvestri (2017; 2018) will be important in providing some feminist criminology and policing insights.

Critical theory will also be supplemented by real-world examples too from news sources in order to help illustrate points further and to explore how the theory fits with policing practice. In the case of the empirical research in relation to the twenty-three policewomen's experiences discussed in Chapter 2, this critical feminist lens will be vital in uncovering and illustrating the same arguments about whether women officers are as good as their male colleagues and can do the same job as well. Unfortunately, this data does not include data from Black, Asian and Minority Ethnic (BAME) officers, and this as well as officer sexuality and disability are areas where I hope to research to address this research limitation in the future. I will, however, use some examples within the media which illustrate problems with racism, misogyny, and policing within this work. Within this book I will also examine suggestions that *as* women they bring something different to the role of police officer (Brown and Heidensohn, 2000).

Next, we will explore whether the disciplinary records for female officers differ from those of male officers in three force areas over a period of five years, and any similarities or differences in this Freedom of Information (FOI) data will be explored in relation to the place of women in the police. This is quite a departure from research which tends to focus on the police–citizen interaction and gendered behaviour of officers (Rabe-Hemp, 2008a; Barnes, Beaulieu, and Saxton, 2017), to focus on their own disciplinary offences, which illustrates a novel methodological approach, though this is not unproblematic either. Discussions about police officers, their ethical stance and behaviours have been researched and continue to be explored more recently as they remain important indicators of policing currently and this impacts on issues of legitimacy (Westmarland and Rowe, 2018). Chapter 3 offers

Introduction 5

a new approach to exploring policemen and policewomen's engagement in disciplinary behaviours in order to examine whether these differ and what this may mean. In utilising these different approaches to researching the police, I hope this book will reinvigorate scholarship in relation to women and policing and push the boundaries in exploring solutions to the challenges faced by policing in society.

Finally, the book will consider some of the current challenges that policing faces and potential shifts in policing styles, and whether, as Brown and Silvestri (2020) found, these shifts in styles are fragile. Recent reports about policewomen's experiences of policing in England and Wales as well as some indicators from the US and Australia will be of note to illustrate similarities, while remaining mindful of the huge differences with policing within those international comparisons. The final chapter will conclude that a continued human rights and equal opportunities approach and ideas from Wollstonecraft remain vital in informing a review of policing through an intersectional feminist and inclusive approach. This approach will be important in rebuilding trust, both for those working within the police as well as for the communities they serve. After the death of George Floyd at the hands of US police, and the rise of the social and political movement #BlackLivesMatter in America, which went global with protests against incidents of police brutality and racially motivated violence, the public require justice (Day, 2019). Change is sought from communities in regard to BAME representation and much better and fairer policing practice in relation to all communities served by the police. This is true in England and Wales, too, as the highest-ranking BAME female officer, Nusrit Mehtab, quit her superintendent role with the Metropolitan Police Service (MPS) in 2021, citing decades of racial discrimination, and this is 21 years after the *Macpherson Report* had sought changes in relation to these issues after the brutal murder of Stephen Lawrence (Loftus, 2008; Newman, 2021). Current figures for BAME police officers show a small and slow moving rise in the right direction at 6.8 per cent nationally in England and Wales (Police Workforce 2020), but with a massive way to go in contrast to the MPS target of 40 per cent (Newman, 2021). In a similar way, while the MPS declares a commitment to gender equality of 50:50, the aim of closing the gender gap in senior leadership by 2020 (BAWP, 2019) will not be helped by Mehtab leaving the force. While setting dates to see change is important, I suggest it will be important to see a structured road map and strategies in place for dealing with backlash towards the plans to gain this equality. Loftus' (2008) suggestion that fears about being disciplined, rather than actual challenge and change to racism within policing after Macpherson, appears a credible argument

6 *Introduction*

in line with statistical evidence about recruitment as well as retention of BAME officers. The conclusion I arrive at is that an intersectional analysis of policing is required to move away from the inequality within policing which is currently holding the service back. Much more research is required in England and Wales. Kimberlé Crenshaw (2017) explained the benefit of an intersectional approach to inequalities and reflected upon these at the Columbia Law School, 2017. She suggested that as a lens this approach acknowledges all of the differences such as race, gender, class, and sexuality, and explores how their oppression intersects. Policing in England and Wales could benefit from such an intersectional analysis on all fronts cited. Crenshaw's (1989) concerns with collective action approaches in order to address those who are most disadvantaged transforms the redress of the inequalities by exploring all of the intersections at which these inequalities take place in order to challenge them and is a useful lens to use to explore the inequalities in policing. It is time in England and Wales to move from equality sound bites in relation to BAME representation and gender equality, to practical developments to effect change in policing. The promise of real transformative change from current and recent policies by examining the gender and pensions wage gaps, and the lack of females across the different ranks in the service are important to note, as well as the dismal numbers of BAME officers appointed and retained across policing, with an exploration of culture from disciplinary records, will be fundamental in moving policing policy to where policing practice needs to be for officers and citizens in the future. Laverick and Cain (2015) noted the importance of flexible working practices to retain older female officers, who may have caring roles, as well as having their own health needs to be met. Laverick, Joyce, Calvey, and Cain (2019) also brought the issue of women officers and their experiences of the menopause to the fore in considering how to keep this wealth of experience within policing. These calls for structural support for female officers can be seen as providing the basis for an equal playing field. Equality which recognises the different roles that women disproportionately have, has often been missing for policewomen, who mirror women within the wider society and often have a disproportionate care burden in relation to children and elderly family members (Laverick and Cain, 2015). Given the strides forwards in terms of the numbers of women in policing, it should not be the case in 2021 that we also see the highest-ranking BAME female officer leave policing in England and Wales citing decades of discrimination, a toxic environment, and a battle at every rank, not just for her but for all BAME officers (Newman, 2021). After watching 'Red, White and Blue' on the BBC by award-winning director Steve McQueen in recent months, which told the true story of Leroy Logan's attempt to change police attitudes of racism from within the police service (BBC Small Axe, 2020), I do wonder whether real inroads have been made in relation to racism when we see reports of police officers who took selfies with black women who had been murdered in London 2020 (Bashir, 2020). This is a prime example of the way in which class, gender, and race can be areas of intersecting oppression. While the Small Axe series of five films were set between the 1960s and 1980s in London, Mehtab's lived experience of the impact of racism now in policing in the MPS culminated in her complaint in 2021, and continues this same theme. While her case for constructive dismissal is ongoing, she contradicts Commissioner Cressida Dick's assertion that the MPS is not institutionally racist, as well as her view this is not a helpful term. Mehtab told Channel 4 news that the inexplicable disproportionality illustrated the institutional racism and structural bias which can be seen across recruitment, retention, misconduct, and lack of promotion. Mehtab suggested that Dick should go and the narrative should change so that 'institutional racism' should be admitted (Newman, 2021). Commissioner Cressida Dick was the first female to become commissioner of the MPS in 2017 (Silvestri 2018). Silvestri noted that even with the first female commissioner in 180 years, police leadership remains the preserve of white men (Silvestri, 2018: 310); however, this is even more pronounced and troubling with the resignation of Mehtab in 2021, almost four years after Dick was first appointed.

1 Wollstonecraft, the 'nature of woman', and women entering the police

This chapter will explore ideas about feminism using an historical and chronological approach, beginning with some of the founding ideas of feminist theory and a textual analysis. This approach will use Mary Wollstonecraft's ideas and written words as a resource for challenging and examining patriarchal gender norms as they are unreflectively institutionalised in male-dominated professions such as policing. Wollstonecraft encountered various arguments about the difference of women to men which would limit their role to maternal and domestic issues, just as the first policewomen would have their role limited to caring for women and children by the use of similar difference arguments about their nature. Unfairness, inequality, and injustice were all critically explored by Wollstonecraft in relation to her century and women's place within that, regardless of the abuse she would face by many male and female peers, just as policewomen have had to challenge and address these same ideas in order to extend their limited policing role. One example of this challenge from policewomen was their resistance to the female uniforms, which did not fit and made their job more difficult, even though they were heavily criticised for this by their male superiors, and they also variously challenged stereotypes about their natural strengths and weaknesses in relation to policing practice (Cunningham and Ramshaw, 2020).

Wollstonecraft had been a great critic and challenge to the patriarchal dimensions of British law, and added her ideas of a good way and a just society within her works. She knew first-hand that to be a companion or teacher was about the only legitimate way for a woman to earn a living, and she had done both, but she also noted the illegitimate ways women were forced to engage in for survival. In her *Thoughts on the Education of Daughters* (1787) she explained that

> Few are the modes of earning a subsistence, and those very humiliating. Perhaps to be a humble companion to some rich old cousin,

DOI: 10.4324/9781003149156-2

Wollstonecraft, the 'nature of woman' 9

or what is still worse, to live with strangers [...] Above the servants, yet considered by them as a spy, and ever reminded of her inferiority when in conversation with the superiors.

(Wollstonecraft 1787/1989: 25)

Wollstonecraft made explicit the idea of equality of the sexes to allow the chance for women to be involved in work and ideas beyond marriage and motherhood. She also provided a powerful critique of marriage and the problems associated with it. Marriage can lead to all kinds of abuse, according to Wollstonecraft, and she explains that asylums and magdalens are not useful remedies for prostitutes when 'It is justice, not charity, that is wanting in the world' (Wollstonecraft, 1792/1994:143). Within such cases Wollstonecraft recognises the injustice for such women, where 'prostitution becomes her only refuge, and the character is quickly depraved by circumstances over which the poor wretch has little power' (Wollstonecraft, 1792/1994: 143).

During the eighteenth century in England, women were denied access to legal or political power since their whole legal status was subsumed either by their fathers or, upon marriage, by their husbands. Perkin (2002: 1) suggests that the subjection of women was enshrined in English law and custom for 900 years, but that the common law reflected rather than caused the subjection, which she suggests was rooted in the physical and political reality of that time. Women were excluded from the political, public sphere, from citizenship and the right to participate within the public realm. As Wollstonecraft herself explained, women did, however, have criminal status when they transgressed the law. Wollstonecraft was keenly aware of some of the issues which would be raised by working within male-dominated professions such as policing. She was aware of the predicament that women face in male-dominated careers just as she had herself faced fear, discrimination, and prejudice about women getting involved with politics and pamphlet writing. Tomalin explains that Horace Walpole had called Wollstonecraft a hyena in petticoats (Tomalin, 1992: 142), which can be contrasted with names levelled at policewomen as 'split arses' or 'a dull tart' centuries later (Cunningham and Ramshaw, 2020). Wollstonecraft was very aware of the inequalities for women such as primogeniture and the reality within the eighteenth century that

Anatomy determined one's destiny, and men were designed to be on top [...] High public office, the professions, the universities and the Church were closed to women [...] they were as far as possible to depend on men.

(Ferguson, 1992: 22)

10 *Wollstonecraft, the 'nature of woman'*

Her rebuttal of her contemporary male thinkers' versions of the 'nature of woman' will be insightful in illustrating how different and radical her stance was, as well as illustrating how these notions of the nature of woman have prevailed within the policing profession today. The primary source historical texts of Wollstonecraft and her peers alongside contemporary criminological studies will be used to explore early ideas about what we may now term feminist principles from the eighteenth century, to investigate their use in the twentieth and twenty-first centuries, and in the specific field of women in policing using a feminist informed discourse analysis. Works by Alison Woodeson (1993), by Louise A. Jackson (2006), and by Joan W. Scott (1988) regarding issues of difference and sameness for feminists will be invaluable resources to discuss the historical integration of women into policing in England and Wales, along with exploring the use of prejudicial ideas about their 'nature'. Later we will also examine the idea that policing has been built around an ideal male officer and that women cannot therefore fit this model as well as men can, Silvestri explained this using the example of the different experiences of time for policemen and policewomen (Silvestri, 2017; 2018).

Wollstonecraft (1759–1797)

In 2021 it is now 262 years since the birth of Mary Wollstonecraft, whose ideas informed what we would now consider feminism, ideas such as education for all, equal human rights, and citizenship. Hunt-Botting and Carey (2004) use the term 'proto-feminist philosophy' in relation to Wollstonecraft, since it is problematic to label her or her philosophy 'feminist' as the word and movement did not exist at this time (Hunt-Botting and Carey, 2004: 708). While we may not be able to label Wollstonecraft feminist, Gunther-Canada (2001) suggests

> Mary Wollstonecraft is often considered the mother of modern feminism because she was the first to form a model of citizenship in which the political subjectivity of the woman herself was the basis of her rights and duties as a citizen.
>
> (Gunther-Canada, 2001: 122)

Bryson suggests that Wollstonecraft established the principles which led to later campaigns for universal suffrage and eventually to the demand for equal participation with men in the worlds of politics and paid employment (Bryson, 1992: 23). Bee Rowlatt, activist, writer, and journalist, has written about Wollstonecraft in her play *An Amazon*

Wollstonecraft, the 'nature of woman' 11

Stept Out (2019) as well as following her journey in her award-winning book *In Search of Mary: The Mother of All Journeys* (2016), and has campaigned and fought for a statue to commemorate Wollstonecraft's life and works in London. Bee suggests that Wollstonecraft is the foremother of modern feminism (Maryonthegreen, 2020). While the sculpture of the spirit of Wollstonecraft by artist Maggi Hambling CBE was initially seen as an affront by some (Thorpe, 2020), it is arguably fitting that this remarkable and fabulous celebration of the spirit of Wollstonecraft, who was also seen as a contentious character in her own time and for centuries later, was undertaken by a pioneer within the art world now who still subverts expectations. The statue was welcomed and unveiled in an online celebration, due to the continued COVID-19 pandemic, on November 10, 2020 (www.maryonthegreen.org/latestnews.shtml, 2020), and I cannot wait to visit it once restrictions ease.

When considering the question of what Wollstonecraft's ideas can add to this study, it is important to highlight what her works do and how they are resonant for exploring the place of women in general in society and in particular in policing. Wollstonecraft was writing in the eighteenth century in England and she attempts to trace women and the construction of gender throughout the history of Western political thought. This can be viewed as a very early concern about gender in a way which has been continued much more recently by many feminist theorists including Offen (2000), Green (1995), and Akkerman and Stuurman (1998). In contrast, and to illustrate her originality, Wollstonecraft's peers do not provide this element to their examination of gender. Secondly, Wollstonecraft attempts within her work to change attitudes from a conception either of women as weak, emotional, and childlike, *or* as devious and sexually powerful, therefore needing containment. She critiques the effects of the socialisation of women, which maintains this situation in her society, seeing it as harmful to men and women. Thirdly, according to Wollstonecraft, women do not know what their true nature is either, but she argues when they are made aware of this and do recognise it, things will change. In this way she is one of a few authors who saw significant potential in women. Fourthly, Wollstonecraft argues for practical policy changes to allow women education and civil status to follow the attitudinal changes that she had argued for. Finally, and again like a few of her contemporary thinkers, Wollstonecraft recognises that women have the capacity and right of citizenship and further opportunities associated with this. Marie-Jean Caritat Condorcet (in McLean and Hewitt, 1994) and De Gouges (in Levy, Applewhite, and Johnson, 1980) in France would be exceptions to this idea rather than the rule. It is quite striking to see the arguments about the nature of woman from

12   *Wollstonecraft, the 'nature of woman'*

Wollstonecraft's era in the eighteenth century, yet that still remain in contemporary discussions about policewomen. Having a background in both Wollstonecraft and policing allows me this critical interpretation or perspective about women and policing.

When researching the works of historical figures like Wollstonecraft using their primary sources, it is important to make the research methods clear to allow the reader of your research to make some judgement about you and your work. Millen (1997), Lather (1988), McRobbie (1982), and Harding (1987; 1991) have provided huge insight into opening up the researcher's position to the reader of the research. An explicit and brief explanation of the researcher's position allows for questions, criticism, and acceptance of this position and the effects of this upon the research itself. The suggestion of an attempt at objectivity, together with the researcher's subjectivity and contextual understanding from feminist methodologies, also avoids the postmodern claim of the uniqueness of research, which lacks reproducibility, or application to other situations.

In order to address the need for a disclosure of some subjectivity of the researcher, I can explain that I wrote my PhD dissertation on Wollstonecraft's works and her contemporaries, and that my research is feminist and is to some extent informed by my own experiences. However, this does not mean the research will be purely subjective but that it will apply a feminist lens to allow a critical exploration of the place of women in the male organisation of policing which keeps women disadvantaged within it. This research also notes problems that a hypermasculine police culture will have on male as well as female officers. This study comes from a feminist perspective in recognising and illustrating the disadvantage that women face within this and other areas of life, and seeks to challenge this position. bell hooks (2000) discusses her earlier definition of feminism to explain that both men and women will benefit from it: 'Feminism is a movement to end sexism, sexist exploitation, and oppression' (hooks, 2000: viii). She explains that men who benefit the most from this system will be released through feminism from the 'bondage of patriarchy' (hooks, 2000: ix) and that her book is for them as well as women. This is similar to arguments put forward by Wollstonecraft about everyone benefiting from ending the oppression of women, and society becoming fairer and more ethical, and it can be argued that this book is also for all of the police family without distinction of sex, ethnicity, sexuality, disability, or rank, to consider and take it into account in their negotiation of their own policing role and style, as well as for academia. Sapiro (1992: 258–9) suggests that feminism involves:

Wollstonecraft, the 'nature of woman' 13

- An opposition to gender hierarchy
- A recognition that such a hierarchy exists
- Women's position as socially constructed
- A challenge to end this

Wollstonecraft's works certainly fit within this definition of feminism as do her equality and human rights arguments. In terms of feminist epistemology, Wollstonecraft was also one of a very limited number of women to include herself as a 'knower' alongside her male contemporaries. This study, therefore, provides comparative studies of Wollstonecraft's work with her peers such as Jean-Jacques Rousseau (1712–1778) and Edmund Burke (1729–1797). Wollstonecraft, by publishing her works, was one of a limited number of women who declared herself a knower within the male-dominated field of political philosophy. She and her work were met with hostility as women were told by male authorities that they would be corrupted by reading this work. The Reverend Richard Polwhele considered Wollstonecraft's death in childbirth as richly deserved, as he heard of her first child born out of wedlock, and he urged others not to read her corrupting works (Rogers, 1982: 218). The importance of Wollstonecraft in relation to feminist epistemology can be further illustrated by the knowledge that *A Vindication* was published in Spain and was made to look as though it had been written by a man (Kitts, 1994: 353). Centuries later, Wollstonecraft was still considered a tainted example of feminism by both women and men, while it was men 'who would go forth to reason and rule in the political realm' (Coote and Pattulo, 1990: 31). hooks (2000) illustrates that this situation continues in relation to feminist ideas and the very word 'feminism' constantly seems to require re-vindicating. She argues this misconception of feminism is perpetuated by the patriarchal modern mass media, so that feminism remains an 'f' word for many who still associate angry women who are anti-men with feminism (hooks, 2000: 1). Research about police culture as hypermasculine, with entrenched, outdated views about the nature of woman, has been illustrated as resistant to change in terms of allowing women to enter policing and has not easily yielded (Brown and Heidensohn, 2000;15). Sexism, as Reiner argued, has remained in the machismo of police culture (Reiner, 1992). Telling police officers, even now, that feminism would be useful in productive police practice would, I think, at best be met with cynicism, a wry smile, and possibly claims of political correctness gone mad from female and male officers. This is not simply the case in relation to police officers. Some of my undergraduate students hold similar views regarding the use of feminism. Feminism within society, not just within

14 *Wollstonecraft, the 'nature of woman'*

policing, has negative connotations, and it will remain a tough ask to consider the benefits of a feminist review of policing. Even with these acknowledgements, an intersectional feminist review of policing is what is needed.

Millen (1997) illustrated a shift in social scientific research in recent years from a prescriptive and orthodox methodology, to ways in which feminists can operate within the social sciences with integrity. This suggestion is not an attempt to fully reconstruct theory to uncover authorial intention, but to fill in what we do know and provide proof and arguments for what we believe to be a representative account. A major shift can be seen in the explanation to readers that this is an interpretation and to also provide some indication of who is actually undertaking the interpretation. This is also consistent with King's (1985) views about history never being subject to total reconstruction. As a researcher, I use Wollstonecraft's words to illustrate that I am not misreading or misrepresenting her ideas, which allows some objectivity, as this also allows the reader to make their own conclusions regarding Wollstonecraft. While I attempt to offer analysis and argument, I am also keenly aware of my own support of issues such as rights for women and of Wollstonecraft generally. I hope many readers will pick up Wollstonecraft's work and add their own interpretations and understanding to the body of work on Wollstonecraft too. After working in higher education for over two decades I am also keenly aware that policing is not the only institution which requires cultural shifts in order to allow women to reach their full potential, and many of the arguments about policing culture can similarly be made in relation to educational institutions too, especially given the neoliberal ideas which have embraced the marketisation of education and the view of students as consumers. Wollstonecraft deals with the kinds of issues that contemporary feminists are still concerned with, such as whether women are the same as men and can do the same types of job, or whether they are different and are unable to do what men can do, but have other 'special' abilities to bring to the role, which are ideas warranting further attention.

The 'nature' of woman

Wollstonecraft had a huge effect on what women were able to argue for in the years which followed, since she provided a gendered critique of the situation of woman within her century. Even though Wollstonecraft is often not credited for her ideas and influence, the ideas that she wrestled with in the eighteenth century can still be seen to be having an impact on

Wollstonecraft, the 'nature of woman' 15

contemporary women and their work as well as their relationship with the state. Wollstonecraft argued against a special, sexual character of woman and argued that women were like men, rational beings with souls who were capable of being involved in questions of justice. Writers such as Moller-Okin (1979), Elshtain (1981), Kennedy and Mendus (1987), Bryson (1992), and Coole (1993), amongst others, have examined the ways that women and their supposed natural abilities have been misrepresented throughout the history of political theory as well as investigated and provided insight into women's participation throughout history. Importantly, the prevailing notions of woman as either weak or as dangerous, from Wollstonecraft's male contemporary thinkers Burke and Rousseau respectively, would relegate the place of woman to the private realm. Moller-Okin (1991) explains that theories of justice are mostly concerned with whether, how, and why persons should be treated differently from each other. She suggests that traditionally sex has been viewed as a clear legitimiser of different rights and restrictions, and that in the main most have not questioned this subordination of women in political theory (Moller-Okin, 1991: 181). Throughout history, when the role of women was addressed within political theory by its male practitioners, women were assigned an inferior role to men with women's allotted sphere in the domestic/private and men's in the political/public, and I will illustrate these conclusions in due course.

Sameness and difference dilemma

Joan W. Scott's (1988) work is fascinating, because she is interested in history, thinkers in the French Revolution, and the larger question of equality versus difference, or as Pateman (1988) calls it, 'Wollstonecraft's dilemma', as I also am. For Scott, the resolution of what she terms the 'difference dilemma' cannot be reached through either ignoring or embracing difference (Scott, 1988: 48). For Scott (1988), the critical position for feminists consists of two moves, first a systematic criticism of operations of categorical difference and refusal of this ultimate 'truth', and second, that this refusal is not in the name of equality or sameness. This refusal is for Scott in the name of an equality that rests on differences, to disrupt the binary opposition of the dichotomy of sameness and difference (Scott, 1988: 48). While we will see that Wollstonecraft had to tread a precarious path to oppose both of the ideas about difference in her era in order to embrace equality, Scott's work is not limited by this dilemma that Wollstonecraft faced. Wollstonecraft had to make her appeals of equality based on sameness of humans, while Scott (1988) was free in terms of the conclusions she could embrace. Scott suggested resolution to the dilemma to allow inclusiveness of difference within equality,

16 *Wollstonecraft, the 'nature of woman'*

disrupting the binary opposition of the dichotomy of the sameness and difference arguments, witnessed since Wollstonecraft's era. These arguments of sameness and difference have remained current, have even reinvigorated debates about sexuality and equality legislation (Chávez, Nair, and Conrad, 2015), and can clearly still also be seen within the arena of women and policing literature (Wilkinson and Froyland,1996). Along with the ideas of Scott (1988), we will examine these arguments as they develop further within Chapter 2.

Rather than Scott's (1988) call to avoid tracing the use of sameness and difference in relation to women, Barbara Taylor's (1983) *Eve and the New Jerusalem*, and Karen Green's (1995) *The Woman of Reason* are examples of works which have concentrated on retracing women's nature and position throughout history and political philosophy. I suggest that seeing these arguments and tracing what they mean for women, especially in relation to policewomen, provides further understanding of how policewomen make sense of their own role and identity, and helps illustrate how both of these arguments have been used in relation to policewomen. My contention regarding Wollstonecraft's dilemma includes the realisation that she treads a precarious path between two major misconceptions of woman, both of which have historically resulted in women's explicit exclusion from citizenship. She needs to avoid both explanations of difference and argue about the commonality of men and women as humans, with rationality and the possibility to progress. Wollstonecraft has to challenge the conception of woman as different – essentially a weak and childlike creature – which was put forward by Burke in his *Enquiry into the Sublime and The Beautiful* (1757). This conception of woman offered by Burke requires that men should paternalistically care for this weak creature, and that women's rights need to be looked after by their (male) father and then husband, rather than women having rights of their own. The other second major misconception of woman was that provided by Rousseau. Like classical Greek thinkers, and adopted by Machiavelli in the Renaissance, Rousseau also suggested that woman's nature was different (Coole, 1993). For Rousseau, this difference was not simply that they were weak but also that they were dangerous to the state. He suggested they were sexually powerful and devious. Such ideas denied women citizenship on the grounds that their nature did not suit them for a role within the public sphere and that their role within the private sphere was of vital importance to the (male) citizens and the state. Wollstonecraft challenges both of these damaging ideas relating to the nature of woman within both her A *Vindication of the Rights of Men* and A *Vindication of the Rights of Woman*. It was not until late 1791

Wollstonecraft, the 'nature of woman' 17

or early 1792 when Wollstonecraft wrote *A Vindication of the Rights of Woman*, and dedicated it to France's foreign minister, Charles Maurice de Talleyrand-Périgord, as an attempt to persuade him to extend the right of education from men in France to also include Frenchwomen. She suggested to Talleyrand that the abstract rights of men should be extended to women, and she illustrated that the argument that they only apply to men was irrational, 'that to see one half of the human race excluded by the other from all participation of government, was a political phenomenon that, according to abstract principles, it was impossible to explain' (Wollstonecraft 1792/1994: 66). Wollstonecraft attempted to persuade women, too, that realising their potential and enjoying education was good for them. She argued education would help women enjoy fulfilling relationships with husbands. She also argued that this would benefit men too, society generally, and allow for progress. She changed the way in which she argued her main points, but the main points remain and can be illustrated within and across the body of all of her works. In her *Letters* she mentioned the oppression of women servants by their masters and wrote,

> Still harping on the same subject, you will exclaim – How can I avoid it, when most of the struggles on an eventful life have been occasioned by the oppressed state of my sex: we reason deeply, when we forcibly feel.
>
> (Wollstonecraft, 1796/1987: 171)

Woman as different and weak

The first conception of woman as different, in contrast to the ideas of Rousseau, was provided by thinkers like John Locke and Edmund Burke (Coole, 1993). Locke had explained that rights are a natural part of being human and he used arguments based on rights to oppose the divine rights of the monarch (Coole, 1993). He also argued that mothers as well as fathers have domain over children until they reach adulthood, and opposed Sir Robert Filmer's *Patriarcha* (1680), which had celebrated the divine rights of kings and patriarchal family relations (Elshtain, 1981). Locke, however, still argued that traditionally women have been subject to their husbands, and that in property disputes husbands should be heeded because they are stronger and more able than women. This work continued the 'woman as different and weak' perspective that is apparent in Western political philosophy. Burke was to develop this further, and Wollstonecraft sought to overturn it. Wollstonecraft examined Burke's *Enquiry Concerning the Origin of Our Ideas of the Sublime and the*

18   *Wollstonecraft, the 'nature of woman'*

Beautiful where he had suggested that women were 'little, smooth, delicate, fair creatures, never designed that they should exercise their reason', but taught they "should lisp, to totter in their walk and nick-name God's creatures" (Burke in Barker-Benfield, 1989: 105). She responded to his notions about the nature of woman by arguing,

> you have clearly proved that one half of the human species, at least, have not souls; and that Nature, by making women *little, smooth, delicate, fair* creatures, never designed that they should exercise their reason to acquire the virtues that produce opposite, if not contradictory, feelings.
>
> (Wollstonecraft, 1790/1994: 46; italics in original)

Wollstonecraft would not accept this view of the nature of woman, nor that women were not equal with men in terms of rationality, and she was certainly not happy to accept that women should spend their time trying to please male observers. She argued this type of weak woman would actually suit the libertine. She also suggested that the rich would enjoy Burke's work as, *'The rights of men* are grating sounds that set their teeth on edge' (Wollstonecraft, 1790/1994: 53). She was to call for fundamental changes to the perception of what it meant to be a 'woman'. What she did go on to do was to use her male contemporaries' broad arguments, which sounded all-inclusive and democratic, just as those from Thomas Paine and John Locke had done, in order to claim the same civil rights for women in her second *Vindication*. This difference is fundamental and illustrates her rejection of contemporary views of the most radical voices in England at this time in relation to the rights of man. In terms of her political philosophy, it illustrates what many of those radicals were arguing for and shows that this did not go far enough for Wollstonecraft, who can therefore be seen as more radical than many others within this group. The first step would be a massive shift in the conception of woman from Burke's ideal of those weak beings tottering and nicknaming God's creatures which she began to critique in her first *Vindication*. She decried all prescriptive methods of maintaining male supremacy, especially by keeping women in a state of childhood, as Burke had suggested. She illustrated how women were socialised,

> Women are told from their infancy, and taught by the example of their mothers, that a little knowledge of human weakness, justly termed cunning, softness or temper, outward obedience, and a scrupulous attention to a puerile kind of propriety, will obtain for them

Wollstonecraft, the 'nature of woman' 19

the protection of a man; and should they be beautiful, everything else is needless, for, at least twenty years of their lives.

(Wollstonecraft 1792/1994: 83)

In her *A Vindication of the Rights of Men*, Wollstonecraft had refuted Burke's dependence on tradition and emotion, and had suggested that this prevented rational debate (Wollstonecraft, 1790/1994: 8). Denying men or women their natural rights in this way was insulting, according to Wollstonecraft. It is the avoidance of these two conceptions of woman which underpins Wollstonecraft's argument based around the sameness of women with men within civil society. It is Wollstonecraft's attempt to navigate between these ideas about the nature of woman in order to provide a new conception of woman which leads ultimately to what Pateman (1988) terms 'Wollstonecraft's dilemma', which would require the argument about the inclusion of difference in the equal treatment of women from Scott (Scott 1988).

Woman as different and dangerous

Equally debilitating and persistent was the conception of woman as dangerous within political philosophy which can be traced back to Plato and Aristotle through to the Renaissance and Machiavelli, and is investigated thoroughly by Moller-Okin (1979), Elshtain (1981), Kennedy and Mendus (1987), Bryson (1992), and Coole (1993). While Christianity had sowed the seed of equality before God, thinkers such as Aristotle, Machiavelli, and Rousseau added the 'threat' dimension to woman's supposed 'nature'. She was different, devious, and potentially dangerous according to them and required strict control within the family and society from an early age.

Wollstonecraft was one of the most severe contemporary critics of Rousseau, and *A Vindication of the Rights of Woman* criticises at some length Rousseau's conception of the nature of woman and his proposed treatment of them. Within this work Wollstonecraft undertook a scathing attack on Rousseau's misguided notions about the nature of woman, and her frustration and sarcasm can clearly be seen within it. At the same time as he suggested the control of women within society, Rousseau radically asserted the rights of man and stressed the importance of man's independence, especially in education. In *A Discourse on the Origin of Inequality* (1755) he provided a hypothetical state of nature which diametrically opposed the earlier thinking which had centred on the fall of man and original sin. He argued that 'man is naturally good, and only by institutions is he made bad' – the antithesis of the doctrine

20 *Wollstonecraft, the 'nature of woman'*

of original sin and salvation through the church (Russell, 1961: 663). In his *Social Contract* (1762), Rousseau illustrated his shift from his contemporaries such as Denis Diderot who, like Francis Bacon, had a strong optimistic belief in science and progress, 'Rousseau attacked all these Baconian notions. Science was not saving us; it was bringing moral ruin on us. Progress was an illusion' (Cranston, 1968: 16). This Baconian influence is certainly easily found within Wollstonecraft's and Condorcet's work, and it therefore marks one point of departure between these contemporaries and Rousseau's ideas on Wollstonecraft.

The independence of man in the writings of Rousseau is a central theme. People within his hypothetical state of nature are considered equal, no one possesses authority over another, and the sexes are not differentiated, since each is seen as naturally having similar status. However, according to Rousseau this situation changed when people left the state of nature in order to enter civil society for self-preservation. It was within society, argued Rousseau, where people were provided with the opportunity of reaching their full potential to reason as well as realising their moral potential. It is also within society that women began to become more dependent because they now bore more children, and this biological difference, he suggested, led to the situation where they were less and less able to provide for and protect themselves. Rousseau and Wollstonecraft both had a view of women as providing a very useful role as mothers, however for Rousseau this motherhood involved servicing the needs of future citizens and citizen husbands. While man's political, moral, and economic independence remained central to Rousseau's thought, he argued that within civil society the sexes adopted different ways of living.

In *The Social Contract* (1762/1968) Rousseau advanced ideas of the good republic and opposed the divine rights of kings. He also retained his ideas about the separate spheres of influence for the different sexes by maintaining that women's political activity would consist of, and be confined to, the 'chaste power' of influencing their husbands. This, he argued, would be in place of formal political or active citizen's rights since Rousseau's conception of women involved the belief that they already held superior sexual, seductive, and psychological powers which they could exert over men.

It was within the pages of *Emile* (1762/1972), however, where Rousseau made his most explicit assertions about the natural differences between the sexes, and their naturally differing roles in society. Rousseau had provided ideas about the superior sexual and psychological resources of women, and he sought to develop his prescription to respond to this conception of women as dangerous within the state, which involved the

Wollstonecraft, the 'nature of woman' 21

control and confinement of women to the domestic sphere. Rousseau explained that 'But for her sex, a woman is a man.... Yet where sex is concerned man and woman are unlike; each is the complement of the other' (Rousseau, 1762/1972: 321). He moved on from this premise of the complementary nature of the sexes to assert that due to the natural differences the education of males and females should also be different. Rousseau argued that, 'When once it is proved that men and women are and ought to be unlike in constitution and in temperament, it follows that their education must be different' (Rousseau, 1762/1972: 326).

Emile was to develop and flourish as independently and autonomously as possible. Sophia, however, was to be educated towards accepting her role in life as a good mother and wife, and was therefore taught to accept her restrictive upbringing. According to Rousseau, a woman's education should lead to certain duties for women,

> To be pleasing in his sight, to win his respect and love, to train him in childhood, to tend him in manhood, to counsel and console, to make his life pleasant and happy, these are the duties of women for all time, and this is what she should be taught while she is young.
> (Rousseau, 1762/1972: 328)

The patriarchal family was natural, according to Rousseau, since the husband/father/active political citizen would have superior skills of strength and reason. This conception of man could be contrasted with the 'natural' incapacities of the passive/mother/non-citizen resulting from her childbearing/rearing role and menstruation, from her different nature. These ideas have ultimately prevailed for all time, as Rousseau suggested, and women are still dealing with these 'duties'. The father/ provider would therefore need to know, and be sure of paternity, and so Rousseau explained that,

> Thus it is not enough that a wife should be faithful; her husband along with his friends and neighbours, must believe in her fidelity; she must be modest, devoted, retiring; she should have the witness not only of a good conscience, but of a good reputation.
> (Rousseau, 1762/1972: 325)

It is this restriction of women, which would check the corruption of the state, and provide good citizens to add to the glory of the state. Unchecked and at political liberty, women would use their difference and devious sexual nature to bring disruption and destruction to the state, given Rousseau's ideas. Reason and the capacity for autonomy

22 *Wollstonecraft, the 'nature of woman'*

were therefore considered only in relation to men, while women were conversely viewed as naturally dependent upon their father's reasoning and later upon that of their husbands. When women would be allowed into the male bastion of policing they would become enforcers for the state, especially in relation to working-class women and their morality. Rousseau had suggested it would be part of women's role to keep a tight rein on children, socializing girls for their complementary or subordinate role within society. This socialization and surveillance of women as suggested by Rousseau, using the dangerous and difference argument in relation to their nature, can be clearly seen centuries later within the role of early female officers in the police. Woodeson suggests these early female officers were more concerned with the morality of young working-class women rather than the sexual double standards at play with the soldiers and men they were mixing with (Woodeson, 1993). In contrast to Rousseau's prescriptions for women, Wollstonecraft argued,

> Strengthen the female mind by enlarging it, and there will be an end to blind obedience; but, as blind obedience is ever sought for by power, tyrants and sensualists are in the right when they endeavour to keep women in the dark, because the former only want slaves, and the latter a play-thing.
>
> (Wollstonecraft, 1792/1994: 90)

Wollstonecraft examined why there was such an unjust situation for women in her society, and suggested there were two possible explanations for this. She did not accept the first explanation, which was the argument of natural difference that had historically excluded women within political theory. She accepted the second explanation that 'civilization has been very partial' (Wollstonecraft, 1790/ 1994: 8). Part of Wollstonecraft's critique of women's place and role within society included her tracing the origins and history of this partial civilization.

Wollstonecraft had to avoid the conception of woman as weak or as dangerous, and as having a nature defined by sex. While both of these conceptions of woman consider woman as weaker than man (lacking the capacity of rationality), one conception was dominated by the suggestion that women were childlike. In the other view, fears were about women's superiority in sexual deviousness, and therefore surveillance was required.

Burke's and Rousseau's conceptions of woman as weak and/or dangerous would however win out historically as the major ideas about the nature of woman, and remain in place, which prevented women from being in the public realm. Centuries would pass while Wollstonecraft's

Wollstonecraft, the 'nature of woman' 23

name and ideas remained tarnished until she was herself vindicated to a great extent in the twentieth century. It is only since 2020 that we have had a statue to commemorate Wollstonecraft's spirit which finally pays tribute to her ideas and their impact. The duties of woman, as suggested by Rousseau, can still clearly be seen as being juggled within policing careers, and certainly issues such as flexible working to retain officers with childcare or other caring responsibilities has been an important factor in supporting the retention of female officers for centuries following Rousseau (Laverick and Cain 2015; VEOHRC, Phase 3, 2019).

Women's integration into policing

It is now important to explore women's integration into policing, and while doing this we will keep one eye on the appearance within this discussion of arguments about women's nature and what the implications of this may be. Brown and Heidensohn (2000) explained that 'The first policewomen were employed on an experimental basis, in part to avoid embarrassments caused by men's behaviour towards women suspects' (Brown and Heidensohn, 2000: 45). Women's integration into policing was, as Jackson (2006) explains, positioned as 'war work', and while this may have initially been seen as advancement, this did not last long. Alison Woodeson (1993) notes their influx during this period, and also notes their 'eagerness to distil moral and social control over women they came into contact with' (Woodeson, 1993: 218). She explores the use of the sexual double standard during the war era with 'the shuffle of righteousness when any lapse by a woman is under discussion – in such a marked contrast to the jovial and man-of-the-world tolerance displayed towards masculine vice' (Woodeson, 1993: 221). Reminiscent of Rousseau's earlier suggestions for women to be watched, the surveillance of women during this era was explored by Woodeson as well as the class interests associated with this, and she noted that alarm bells did not ring until full curfews for women were ordered (Woodeson, 1993: 227).

Suggestions about the 'nature' of woman and the use and abuse of these arguments in relation to women being able to initially join the police will be examined. Jackson explains the integration on grounds of their difference,

> Yet the argument was often won on the grounds of gender difference rather than equal rights: that there was 'a special sphere of usefulness' for policewomen.
>
> (Jackson, 2006:18)

24 *Wollstonecraft, the 'nature of woman'*

The social maternalism concept was effectively used to initially get women into policing.

(Jackson, 2006: 200)

These ideas fit with the conception of woman from Rousseau in which they would be a complement to men and would add their own special usefulness, even though this notion differs from his suggestion of women remaining within the private realm. Jackson goes on to explain that,

It is often argued that the 1920s saw a splitting of feminist ideologies. 'Old' feminists such as Margaret Rhondda and Winifred Holtby continued to advocate equal rights for men and women, believing that gender difference should be eradicated. The 'new' feminism associated with Elanor Rathbone emphasised difference between the sexes and argued that women should be valued for their special role as citizens, which was located in relation to maternity.

(Jackson, 2006: 19–20)

This illustrates both arguments being deployed in campaigns to allow for women in policing but that the emphasis on their special skills seemed to dominate (Jackson, 2006). For policewomen, then, there was 'the need for a careful balancing of the rhetoric of both equality and femininity, and the importance of personal determination and strength of will' (Jackson, 2006: 23). Woodeson (1993) reminds that by the end of World War I there was a decline in women police, 'But the dominant interests had found the excuse they needed for ousting the policewomen by highlighting the social and moral aspects of their work' (Woodeson, 1993: 230). In the post–World War II era essentialist arguments were made again for women officers to deal with juvenile delinquents and child neglect as well as undertake what Jackson terms the dual role in policing of taking statements. 'In the aftermath of the Second World War, policewomen performed a dual role that combined specialist "women's" work with standard "police" work' (Jackson, 2006: 26). Andrew and Lomas (2017) explained how women were able to push their natural boundaries during this period when men were away. So women were also allowed into the male bastion of policing for their social function but also as a moral compass essentially to control women, as state enforcers, at least initially. By the 1960s, senior policewomen were positioning their officers as both equal and different (Jackson, 2006: 41). Laverick (2021) also importantly notes that with full integration there was a loss of this specialist expertise that policewomen had built up, with the impact of this loss being seen in some damning reports

Wollstonecraft, the 'nature of woman' 25

and enquiries since the 1970s. Laverick (2021) notes the work of Reece and Strange (2019), which had seen early concerns about women's integration in relation to women forming relationships with policemen and suspects. This is worth considering in relation to Chapter 3 when we see the kinds of disciplinary offences female and male officers are actually engaged in. Brown explained that research into women and policing increased after the Sex Discrimination Act 1975 and after tribunal cases illustrated a sexist environment and informal quotas which restricted numbers of women officers (Brown, 1998: 265). Brown had argued that it was the inappropriate transposition of stereotype sexual role behaviour into the workplace that accounts for discrimination and sexual harassment (Brown, 1998: 266–7).

Jackson's (2006) note about the inclusion of women based on their difference and, importantly, her raising the idea of feminine moral superiority (Jackson, 2006: 5) are both issues to follow in relation to the ideas surrounding the nature of woman to add to the historical references. Ideas about high ethical and moral standards in relation to women are also worth revisiting in Chapter 3 when we explore women's as well as men's disciplinary offences. These same ideas can be seen in real-world current examples such as in relation to issues which have emerged with the suggestion of female officers taking the lead in public order issues, since they can be seen to behave more ethically in more recent incarnations of the difference argument. The Ian Tomlinson case in the public order policing of the G20 demonstrations in London raised concerns that hypermasculine policing styles would further damage support and legitimacy for policing in England and Wales (Henley, 2009). Decades earlier, Reiner had warned of the loss of legitimacy and trust in policing (1992). Importantly, the incidents which did highlight the inappropriate use of force in these events was recorded by police officers as well as citizens who were protesting and had recorded the pushing of Ian Tomlinson by a police officer, on their mobile phones before he fell and later died (Chadwick, 2018). Heidensohn and Brown (2000) argued that women have been found to operate with different communicative styles, and cite the work of Miller and Braswell (1992), who suggested that women officers do engage in more ethical behaviour (Heidensohn and Brown, 2000: 102), and this was certainly borne out in the policing of the G20 along with suggestions that women should be heading up major policing responses and public order policing (Henley, 2009). Research which tends to focus on the police–citizen interaction and gendered behaviour of officers has become important to explore with Rabe-Hemp's (2008a) study finding that 'Female officers' underutilization of force may actually produce police-citizen encounters that are

26 *Wollstonecraft, the 'nature of woman'*

safer for female officers and the citizens they encounter' (Rabe-Hemp, 2008a: 431). We will examine this issue further in relation to whether women's and men's involvement in disciplinary offences is similar or different in any way later in Chapter 3.

Summary

An understanding of where the deeply entrenched notions and misconceptions about the nature of woman have come from, and how they have been articulated has been discussed. The ability to see these arguments constantly emerging in relation to women allows critique and challenge to such views. Left to flourish, such pervasive and damaging views about what women are and what they can do is devastating for women and emboldening for predatory men, and can have impacts which can be seen as discriminatory right across society and the criminal justice system.

Knowing about the shortcomings of the equality arguments that Wollstonecraft had to use rather than her accepting the crippling effects of difference arguments was paramount in the eighteenth century in England regarding women, and is important to distinguish now in order to pursue inclusion and diversity. I cannot agree with Scott's (1988) suggestion that we should stop tracing these arguments as they developed since they led to the 'difference dilemma', and I would argue that knowing where these come from, and the impact they have had is vital. This knowledge and understanding about the sameness and difference arguments provides a deeper level of understanding of the complexity involved in suggesting resolution of difference and equality arguments which continues in the next chapter. Resolution to Wollstonecraft's dilemma (Pateman, 1988) can only be approached centuries after Wollstonecraft where difference can be included in equality of treatment arguments, for instance (Scott, 1988).

2 Re-emerging arguments about the nature of woman, a re-examination of twenty-three policewomen data and a review of policing in Australia

Introduction

We move on from the discussion in Chapter 1, which has explored historical conceptions of the nature of woman and what these arguments would allow women to do, to the persistence of the arguments about policewomen's sameness or difference to policemen which have continued well into the twenty-first century. These arguments have survived and can be seen to flourish, as will be detailed in this chapter. I will provide an illustration and application of these ideas in revisiting data from an empirical study of policewomen's lived experiences in the twenty-first century, in order to provide an additional layer of analysis to this research (Cunningham and Ramshaw, 2020).

Wilkinson and Froyland's (1996) concerns regarding sameness and difference from the 1990s in Australia will be examined to explore arguments about whether women officers are the same as or different to male officers in arguments reminiscent of Wollstonecraft hundreds of years earlier. The resonance of these ideas with a recent review of policing in Victoria, Australia, which worked with the Human Rights Commission to effect individual and cultural change in policing policy and practice from 2015 will also be illustrated (VEOHRC, 2019). This gap of 25 years will allow an indication of whether there have been any changes within this period.

Finally, discussion about the sameness and difference dilemma will be reconsidered in relation to using an inclusive and transformational approach to resolve the dilemma (Squires, 2007).

Twenty-three women officers' data revisited

Women's integration into policing has been a contested journey and has utilised ideas about the 'nature of woman' in order to begin and to

DOI: 10.4324/9781003149156-3

28 *Re-emerging arguments*

continue to develop on this journey. We also know from a number of studies that these women have had to deal with discrimination, harassment and sexism, not simply at the point of integration but persistently on their journey within their policing role (Brown and Heidensohn, 2000; Brown, 2000; Renzetti, 2013; Silvestri, 2018; Cunningham and Ramshaw 2020). Our understanding about the use of arguments regarding the 'nature of woman' we have seen thus far, can help add further depth and insight to our illustration of the place of women in policing from earlier studies.

The data in this chapter refers to a study of 23 policewomen's lived-experiences of policing in England and Wales that I undertook along with a colleague and took a lead on writing the subsequent article on (Cunningham and Ramshaw, 2020). Here I revisit that data, given the arguments made within this book, with the ideas about sameness and difference found in Wollstonecraft's works in the eighteenth century, but also having illustrated how central these ideas have remained within the initial inclusion of women in policing. Seeing these same ideas variously re-emerging, and persistently remaining within the policing literature currently means that it will be vital to address them and add that further level of analysis to that study. We had taught police officers who had agreed to participate in this study and we utilised a snowballing method to eventually reach 23 women at different levels of rank and experience in policing who candidly answered our questions in face-to-face interviews across England. In this chapter I now will re-evaluate that data with a fresh perspective to seek a new level of analysis about women's inclusion and practice in policing over the four decades of the study. I hope to compare and contrast the findings from that study with those from the *Review of Policing* in Australia, and while noting the differences I hope to explore any commonality of themes. In 2020, our findings had been that disruption (Silvestri, 2018) of the status quo of policing culture happened during periods of unrest, or at least there had been an interruption of this (Loftus, 2008); however, the norm over the four decades remained that of a continued white heterosexist male culture (Cunningham and Ramshaw, 2020). I will explore feminist theory alongside practice as well as take into account the re-emergence, and continued use of ideas about women vis-à-vis their male colleagues in terms of their 'nature' and ability in relation to their policing practice.

Within the data capture of the 23 policewomen over four decades, aspirations to secure justice and 'make a difference' were noted by all the participants as motivation for entering this profession. All of the policewomen had a wealth of experience gained across the four generations that their work covered, and they had all been committed to doing the best job they could possibly do under often incredibly difficult

Re-emerging arguments 29

circumstances. Here, it is important to note the value of the job and the role of police officer, and to acknowledge that not everyone can do this job. While I am providing a critique of policing within this book, this is so that policing can improve in terms of representation, fairness and proportionality in practice, not simply to criticise the police. I was impressed by all of the officers whose employment as officers was informed by their wish to be involved in a police service which sought fairness and justice, and I was surprised by them looking forward to the next unknown workday that they would face. All of the officers had listed communication skills rather than gender, sex or strength as the most important factors within policing and doing a good job, while paradoxically also having had experiences of being limited within their role precisely due to this 'difference' from the male ideal or norm within policing. This treatment due to difference can be seen and illustrated in revisiting the earlier co-written paper as a structural gendered bias in terms of preventing access to specialised policing departments like with the dog or horse section, as these were not historically seen to be appropriate arenas for women officers (Cunningham and Ramshaw, 2020: 32). Secondly, this sex discrimination could include deliberate toxic masculinity, too, at the worst end of the scale, such as within the misogyny of being objectified either through the use of sexist language and 'banter', like being called 'split arses' or by having their image superimposed onto a grossly overweight woman, or being 'tested' by being invited to a strip club by male colleagues after work (Cunningham and Ramshaw, 2020: 33). Similar examples were recently also cited by Nusrit Mehtab in 2021 in her Channel 4 interview where she spoke about her male BAME colleagues who had been exposed to racist discriminatory behaviour by colleagues and where their pictures were also defaced (Newman, 2021), and this contrasts with earlier expectations that explicit racism would be unlikely to happen post-Macpherson (Cunningham and Ramshaw, 2020: 33). This is an area which really does require much further research, as will be detailed within this book where my research analysis from the press informs the space where no BAME officers were included in the earlier study to add further experience and insight. Thirdly, this treatment as different could also be unintentional, as seen more recently by simply still adhering to an idea of the ideal or norm of the officer as male, and not checking that new equipment could be used by both male and female officers with their different body shapes in order to utilise this new technology (Cunningham and Ramshaw, 2020). This continues the research documented by C. Martin (1996), who found that women officers were dissatisfied with the impractical uniform. Reflection on the 2020 data also illustrates that the uniforms had been an insight into the consequences of this 'difference' for policewomen. Wearing stockings, a

30 Re-emerging arguments

pencil skirt and an air hostess-style hat illustrated this difference in practical terms in the study which spanned several decades (Cunningham and Ramshaw, 2020: 29). For men in society as well as the men within policing, this uniform for policewomen, which was similar to that of an air hostess, reflected a fantasy of the attractive policewoman as a sexual commodity or for others as an administrative assistant, often the only woman in the department. Women officers were invariably therefore split arses or dull tarts (Cunningham and Ramshaw, 2020). This difference in uniform was seen to be used by women officers as a site of resistance, with many women sharing their experiences of themselves fighting for sameness in this regard, to be allowed to wear trousers like their male colleagues and sometimes being disciplined for these attempts by their superiors (Cunningham and Ramshaw, 2020: 29–30). Women found it very difficult to do their job well while wearing their police uniform, which was created for policewomen as different. If this was not bad enough for women, their appearance could also lead to questions from superiors about their sexuality too, 'look you've dropped the W, you've had your hair cut really short, you wear a man's tie, are you a lesbian?' (Cunningham and Ramshaw, 2020: 30). In more recent times the uniform has developed in terms of the idea of the 'sameness' of all officers, with all often wearing combat-style trousers and a similar shirt or T-shirt-style tops. The problem of planning for, designing and expecting a policeman in this role continued to be illustrated in using new technology and vests in recent times. The new kit had been designed without taking into account that women were police officers too, who had breasts. This difference was physical and required thought:

> The best laugh was [supervisors] wanted me to wear a headcam last year, your headcam went onto your shoulder and the main power pack went into your pocket. They gave me this special vest to wear […] so I had to make [the pocket] as big as possible and when I did the camera then pointed at my feet. The inspector at the time couldn't understand what was wrong. I said well it's obvious there's no darts in it, it's aimed for men not women, he went bright red. (P3, 2004)
>
> (Cunningham and Ramshaw, 2020: 30)

In the same way that the uniform had been designed for the ideal male officer and the difference was massively pronounced to fit 'woman as different', policing the Miner's strike was an example where the operation had been set up with the ideal male officer in mind by the use of male-only dorms and facilities which would exclude women. During this

Re-emerging arguments 31

era, women were not expected to be at the frontline, and their difference would ensure this did not happen for decades. This experience noted by policewomen did however bring unexpected benefits from the males going to fill such needs since it allowed policewomen opportunities to experience different types of policing that they would not otherwise have been given the chance to do (Cunningham and Ramshaw, 2020: 31). This unexpected by-product of being seen as different and remaining in post while men left to police emergency needs was a positive outcome of the 'difference' arguments. Normally the working out of duties in line with difference from the male officers would mean doing the administrative tasks, being the woman in the office, or even dealing with sexual assault cases when both male and female officers had undergone the training for this (Cunningham and Ramshaw, 2020). The experiences of the women from this data illustrated that these policewomen had to adhere to these outdated notions of what was expected of a woman to a large extent; however, they felt that they were within their rights to protest about the difference in uniforms. Difference within this data was also illustrated by respondents' discussion of their caring role and responsibilities even in the post-equality legislation phase in policing. The ideas of women's usefulness in relation with the social maternalism concept remained, with many of our respondents speaking about being left to look after children in their job, even where they had no children of their own while their male colleagues did have children. This example of 'difference' was more negative and limiting for the policewomen we spoke to.

The officers in this data set had utilised a variety of responses in order to deal with these issues and get on with their main task of policing, which was a job they loved. Responses from the participants included ignoring or explaining unpleasant sexist terminology as 'banter', with one participant suggesting this was useful to prepare her for the real world, or alternatively investigating the culprit of the superimposed picture, then following this with a formal complaint, or highlighting the different body shape in relation to using the bodycams, or joining colleagues at a strip club after work (Cunningham and Ramshaw, 2020). Many studies have examined women officers' use of a variety of tactics to negotiate their role successfully (Heidensohn, 1992: 2002). Reflecting on this data, the nature of woman, and difference and sameness analysis illustrate that these officers dealt with everyday sexism and misogyny while undertaking their policing role to the very best of their abilities.

All of the officers had sought within these difficulties, trials and challenges to get on with their major role of policing in spite of these barriers and being considered different or 'other'. In none of these cases

32 *Re-emerging arguments*

did the women simply passively accept their treatment by their male peers or indeed by their superiors, even where this caused them disciplinary problems. Further analysis and reflection on their experience of policing and arguments which abound and that still impose ideas about 'natural' strengths and weaknesses of policewomen, are very important to continue to note, observe, and critique. These outdated ideas can clearly be seen to impact and provide insight within this data. Gender inequalities such as care responsibilities, childcare burdens, gender wage gaps, pensions, and lack of representation of BAME officers, alongside a lack of women across all levels of policing, remain pertinent issues in policing practice, just as the arguments about sameness and difference persistently remain within society at large and policing, reflected in the policing literature.

Sameness and difference in policing re-emerges

As we saw in Chapter 1, Heidensohn (2002) confirms that initially

> Women's entry into policing in the UK and the USA, and in some European nations and Australia, was promoted in the late nineteenth century and early twentieth century precisely to provide protection to female and juvenile offenders and victims which, it was felt, they did not receive from an all-male force (Carrier 1988; Feinman 1986).
>
> (Heidensohn, 2002: 501)

She also explains the importance of including an examination of gender within studies on policing, suggesting that

> Findings from studies with a gender perspective throw light on the role and position of women in law enforcement, reconstruct the notion of police culture, and form part of the basis for 'modernization' in many agencies around the world.
>
> (Heidensohn, 2002: 502)

Heidensohn (2002) examines some of the different kinds of research undertaken in this field, like Martin's (1980), which was the first major study of female officers and that suggested that both *Police* women and Police *Women* existed from the Washington, DC, study (Heidensohn, 2002: 502). She argued the former competed with their male colleagues, while the latter accepted subordinate roles and did not compete. I would suggest the former had the sameness identity at the forefront too, while the latter internalised a difference perspective to their peers, given the pervasiveness of these ideas on women generally and on policewomen in particular who had entered a very male domain. These conceptions of the nature of women do not occur in a vacuum; rather, they permeate and have been entrenched across different historical periods and been internalised by women and men, and they still continue. If, as a policewoman, your primary notion about yourself is that of being the same as your male peers, you would compete with your male colleagues as POLICE, seeing yourselves as all POLICE together, whereas if your main conception of yourself as a police WOMAN was that of different and perhaps complementary to your policemen peers, then you would be less likely to compete and more likely as a WOMAN to accept the subordinate roles that you had been socialised to accept, so perhaps this provides further insight into why the different types of policewomen exist. Identity is a massive part of a police officer's perception (Skolnick, 2008) and has been explored in detail in many studies about women officers too. Heidensohn also explored Jones's 'Medshire' study in Britain which described both 'traditional' and 'modern' types of woman officers (Heidensohn, 2002: 502). Heidensohn noted her earlier work where she had compared American and British policewomen and had found that in public order situations they used similar tactics to their male counterparts. They were very different in the way they presented themselves, according to Heidensohn, 'developing ways to construct "presences" and demonstrate them in challenging situations' (Heidensohn, 2002: 502). In a later project Brown and Heidensohn (2000) had compared an international sample of policewomen and found, as all earlier studies had, macho cop culture, sexual discrimination and sexual harassment by male officers towards their female counterparts (Heidensohn, 2002: 502), as we ourselves found in 2020 (Cunningham and Ramshaw, 2020).

Wilkinson and Froyland (1996) explained that in Australia during the 1990s women made up 13.5 per cent of sworn police officers (Wilkinson and Froyland, 1996:1). They argued that

> The main issues in the employment of women in policing are:
> * The recruitment of women;
> * The deployment of women as specialists or generalists;
> * The representation of women in senior ranks and management;
> * Police culture and attitudes to women police; and
> * Working conditions.
> (Wilkinson and Froyland, 1996: 1)

34 *Re-emerging arguments*

Arguably, 25 years later, these still remain issues in representation for women and BAME officers in policing in England and Wales today as well as being amongst major findings in the *Review of Policing* in 2015 in Victoria, Australia (VEOHRC, 2019; Cunningham and Ramshaw, 2020), alongside childcare, family commitments, shift work, and the gender and pension wage gap, showing the persistence of these issues not only in policing but also as reflected from within the wider society too.

Wilkinson and Froyland (1996) suggested that female officer numbers illustrated a need to re-examine practices and suggested 'difficulties at the three stages of police recruitment: application, selection and police academy training' (Wilkinson and Froyland, 1996: 1). They called for more research to 'determine whether this is because young women do not see policing as an appropriate occupation for females, or they think that their chances of being selected are poor' (Wilkinson and Froyland, 1996: 1–2). They suggested that further research would inform attempts to recruit women and members of minority groups, and that while it is not essential to have equal numbers of men and women, 'that until a critical mass of women in policing is achieved, it will be difficult to even begin to counter discriminatory attitudes, behaviours and practices against women' (Wilkinson and Froyland, 1996: 3). They argued that while women are in the minority, each individual is visible, her performance public, and her acceptance from males is often conditional. Irving (2009) compares Australia to England and Wales to find that

> In Australia, there was a 70 percent increase in the overall proportion of women in policing in the period 1996 to 2006, considerably higher than the 44 percent increase in England and Wales over a similar period. Currently, exactly the same proportion (23%) of police officers in England and Wales and in Australia are female.
>
> (Irving, 2009, aic.gov.au)

While the number of women officers has continued to rise in England and Wales as well as in Australia, Roman (2020) reports this has not been the case in the United States with figures stuck around 12 per cent.

Women's deployment in traditionally male-oriented occupations raises important issues because officers need to have a range of experience in order to progress through such organisations. Within policing there is a huge amount of lateral police career choices and movement. While Wilkinson and Froyland (1996) found little evidence that women had been discriminated against, this was not the case later with the findings of the *Review of Policing* in Victoria, which began in 2015 (VEOHRC 2019).

Re-emerging arguments 35

In arguments reminiscent of Wollstonecraft's ideas about sameness, Wilkinson and Froyland earlier suggested that in relation to the police,

> If female officers are perceived as less able than male officers to perform policing tasks, they cannot expect to be similarly deployed. Early expectations of women in policing were that they would not succeed in this male-oriented occupation but research has not borne that out. Female officers are considered at least equal to male officers in most areas of police work (Poole and Pogrebin, 1988). They are as effective as males in performing patrol duties (Martin, 1993), and have demonstrated no consistent differences in the quality of their performance in street policing. (Worden, 1993).
>
> (Wilkinson and Froyland, 1996: 3)

Even in terms of the argument around men being physically stronger than women and this having a detrimental effect on women police officers undertaking their task, Wilkinson and Froyland (1996) argued that while the physical nature of policing is often commented upon, research does not always confirm its importance. They provide a research example from England by Brown, Maidment, and Bull (1992) to argue that when 32 sergeants were asked what characteristics they considered most necessary for ten different policing tasks, physical force, physical strength, and physical stature did not feature strongly. This was also the case in terms of the 23 policewomen (Cunningham and Ramshaw, 2020). Appropriate assessment, initiative, and moral and physical courage were seen as more important, with the highest ratings for verbal communication, assessment, effective listening, and consideration of others. Wilkinson and Froyland's discussion of the 'woman as different' approach included the following observation:

> Largely untested stereotypes about women credit them with particular abilities such as sensitivity, people skills and understanding. The implication is that women should not only be permitted to undertake all policing duties engaged in by men, they should be respected and even deployed on the basis of their special abilities (Brown et al. 1992; Martin, 1993; Worden, 1993).
>
> (Wilkinson and Froyland, 1996: 3)

Gregory and Lees (1999) also argued that such statements simply swap one set of stereotypes for another. According to them, the best selection procedures and training mechanisms are required for all officers. Wilkinson and Froyland (1996) go on to cite an ACPO strategic

36 Re-emerging arguments

document (Association of Chief Police Officers, 1990) which had suggested

> policing is about community reassurance as well as law enforcement and should be undertaken with compassion, courteousness and patience. These are attributes which have been particularly associated with women's traditional roles.
>
> (Wilkinson and Froyland, 1996: 3)

In a very similar vein to the question of Wollstonecraft's dilemma, as argued by Pateman (1988), and the difference dilemma by Scott (1988), Wilkinson and Froyland later posited the situation as it applied to women and policing,

> The dilemma, then, is equal or not equal. Do we treat women as equal in all respects, to be deployed regardless of gender or do we accept that certain special characteristics, which some consider are unique to women, make them more able to perform certain tasks? If so, then are they less able to perform than others?
>
> (Wilkinson and Froyland, 1996: 3)

While they do not offer a resolution to this dilemma, they argue that everyone has some special abilities regarding gender, and that in relation to women in policing, the argument of having special abilities or a 'woman as different' approach is counterproductive to functioning as equal police officers, which mirrors the views of the 23 officers who participated, even though paradoxically these same women had experienced harassment or blocked opportunities precisely because they were women (Cunningham and Ramshaw, 2020). Wilkinson and Froyland (1996) went on to consider police culture and attitudes towards women, suggesting some men find women police officers problematic since they see policing tasks as inappropriate for women and see women as incapable of achieving in some situations. They argue that sometimes male officers feel the need to protect women and believe they would not be effective work partners in a brawl, and they suggest British research tends to confirm this. They cite the work of Brown and Campbell (1991), which showed that women officers were steered towards traditionally female tasks, are subject to negative attitudes from older but not younger officers, are seen as lacking in terms of commitment, and are asked more often to undertake activities which require 'people skills' (Wilkinson and Froyland, 1996: 4). They also cited Martin's (1979) research in the United States which suggested female officers were sometimes appointed as token women. Only about one in five patrol officers willingly accepted women partners, and ordinary policemen's attitudes towards policewomen were seen in Balkan's (1988: 33) study as 'uniformly negative' earlier (Wilkinson and Froyland, 1996: 34).

Gregory and Lees explained the men in Jones's study had also insisted that in a violent situation a women officer could put a male officer at risk – either not being able to back him up or because he felt bound, out of chivalry, to protect her and so put himself at risk. This was however countered by one woman police constable (WPC) who claimed women were better at diffusing situations and therefore had less aggressive behaviour to deal with (See Gregory and Lees, 1999: 28). These studies highlight the ideas of women as different and weak in relation to male police officers.

Wilkinson and Froyland argue a difference in attitudes in a study from the Centre for Police Research (1994) which illustrated that sergeants thought women might diffuse situations, and two-thirds thought they should make up about 10 per cent or less in the service. Sergeants argued the police should not do more to make it possible to combine a police career with marriage and children during this time (Wilkinson and Froyland, 1996: 5). Constables, in contrast, indicated no preference in operational partner, thought 20–30 per cent of women should be in the service, and 71 per cent agreed that the service should do more to make it possible to combine a police career with marriage and children (Wilkinson and Froyland, 1996: 5). Wilkinson (1994) found a perceived inflexibility of the organisation to accommodate women trying to balance their roles as mother and police officer to be the principal factor in the decision of Western Australian women to leave policing. This applies to both flexible weekly working arrangements and flexible arrangements for career breaks for childbearing (Wilkinson and Froyland, 1996: 5). It would take until 2015 until issues such as the work-life balance and childcare and shift work would be on the strategic review of challenging these inequalities in Australia (VEOHRC, Phase 3, 2019) where the model of the police officer appears to remain that of a male, and has been questioned. While Wilkinson and Froyland concluded in the 1990s there was no place in Australian policing for any ineffective officers of either gender (Wilkinson and Froyland, 1996: 6), structural discrimination had not been addressed at this point and arguably policing was not at this time ready to accept such challenges. This situation has not changed or become more equal by the twenty-first century for women. Meanwhile back in England and Wales by exploring female and male officers, Dick and Metcalf (2007) found that in '2005 13 per cent of female officers

38 *Re-emerging arguments*

were sergeants compared to twenty-four per cent for male officers (RDS, 2005)' (Dick and Metcalf, 2007: 82). Their study found that 'although the proportion of female officers has increased substantially from 19 per cent in 1999 to 24 per cent in 2005 female officers remain significantly under-represented in senior ranks' (Dick and Metcalf, 2007: 91). Laverick and Cain (2015) also found a need for flexibility in policewomen's careers and their working arrangements in order to retain them, especially if they had care responsibilities with children or parents. By 2007, in England and Wales the figure for women in the police was 23 per cent, as reported by *Newsround*'s '100 Years of Women in the Met' and by 2019 the number had reached a national figure of 30 per cent (Newsround, BBC, 2019), which was heartening to see on the children's BBC *Newsround* site along with the aim of a Metropolitan Police Service (MPS) with a 50:50 gender make-up. With the figures in England and Wales increased to 30 per cent of policewomen (Brown and Silvestri, 2020), it remains to be seen when parity of police officer numbers will be reached in policing and how this will be achieved, as well as how any backlash may be dealt with which may well accompany this. Since the 1980s in England and Wales, and following the recommendations of Lord Scarman's report on disturbances by young people who rioted in deprived areas in England, calls have been made to explore how to make policing more representative of those communities it serves (Scarman, 1981). Racial disadvantage alongside socio-economic disadvantage were seen as elements which had informed the riots along with a mistrust of the police and policing operations (Reiner, 1992). Mapherson's report after the killing of Stephen Lawrence in London continued this call for representation and used the terms 'institutionally racist' to describe the MPS; however, little change in numbers or indeed attitudes and behaviours has been seen. As Jones and Rowe (2015) argued, this fairer representation and diversity in policing is better for communities, as well as adding operational advantages and the promotion of professionalism, ethics, and integrity. These debates, agendas, and policy changes have, however, made few inroads into policing and diversity as yet, according to Jones and Rowe (2015). This is mirrored by Brown and Heidensohn (2000) in relation to the fair passage of women in policing; however, it appears that there is still much to be done on both counts in 2021. Representation still has a long way to go in 2021, as Muir in *The Guardian* explains the situation in relation to BAME officers,

> The Home Office says there were 9,174 BAME police officers on 31 March 2020 – an increase of 842 on the previous year and 7.3% of all officers. But that still represents only just more than half of the

proportion of those it classifies as 'other ethnic groups' in the population. The proportion of senior BAME officers has risen from a paltry 2.8% in 2007 to just 4%.

(Muir, 2021, Black and blue: the secret lives of
BAME police officers | Police | *The Guardian*)

Muir (2021) goes on to explain the need for representation of the population and illustrates the importance of both recruitment and retention of BAME officers,

In London, where 44% of the population is believed to be black or from an ethnic minority, the problem is particularly acute. Sadiq Khan, widely expected to be re-elected as London mayor in May, has called on the Met – which has the most BAME officers of any force: 5,000 out of 32,600 – to raise its target for BAME officers from 19% to 40%. On past performance, that is a huge ask. It is virtually impossible to build diverse, effective forces if too few BAME officers sign up and too many – finding that hardships and unfairness still bedevil their careers – choose to leave.

Gender equality was still described as a long-term aim in 2018 where gender representation in the Met was the third lowest, just above the City of London and Cleveland forces (Dodd, 2018). Even more disturbing are the claims from Black Met Police officers that racism blighted their careers (Dodd and Busby, 2020), and the statistic that in May of last year over four times more black than white people were still stopped and searched in London. Dodd and Busby (2020) suggest that it could take another 100 years before we have a more representative police service, and without it policing legitimacy will remain difficult to attain. Acknowledgement that institutional racism is a problem should be the starting point for change; however, this is not even accepted by Cressida Dick (Newman, 2021), which suggests that transformative change is a long way off for policing.

In terms of women officers and their policing styles, Brown and Heidensohn (2000) argued that 'community policing not only rejects the male policing model but positively embraces feminine qualities as ideal traits for the neighbourhood officer' (Brown and Heidensohn, 2000: 98). They go on to cite Lersch (1998), who argued that women officers were more likely to have a calming effect on police–public encounters and be more effective in diffusing volatile situations (Brown and Heidensohn, 2000: 101). Further, they cite the work of Miller and Braswell (1992), who suggested that women officers do engage in more ethical behaviour

40 Re-emerging arguments

(Brown and Heidensohn, 2000: 102). Policewomen's style of policing was seen as important for maintaining police and citizen relations. By 2009, similar arguments were seen to resurface after the criticism of the hypermasculine and toxic policing tactics of the G20 protests, when Jon Henley (2009) in *The Guardian* suggested that the Met had recently announced a new strategy – that of putting women officers in charge of operations to avoid the violence seen at the G20 protests,

> But there is an acknowledgement within the service here, says one study supervised by Brown, that it needs to 'reconsider its styles and priorities [...] and create a model of policing that is more consultative. The model that has evolved takes on initiatives having the appearance of a more feminised style'.
>
> (Henley, 2009, A force to be reckoned with | Police | *The Guardian*)

After the police shooting and death of Mark Duggan, and the peaceful protest which followed in London in 2011, it became clear to see that police legitimacy had still not been achieved (Lewis, 2011), and the lack of communication and consultation from the police and the Independent Police Complaints Commission (IPCC) was cited as part of the problem, which led to frustration and riots. The male model of policing as tough, crime fighting, physical and aggressive in nature and white (Silvestri, 2017) may be supplemented by a more consultative style which embraces feminine traits; however, trust in the police will need rebuilding over time in BAME communities as this has been a problem for decades, so there will be no quick fix in response. Reiner (1992) argued decades earlier that

> opinion of the police is most negative amongst particular groups, those who are routinely at the receiving end of police powers: the young, males, the economically marginal, especially if they are also black and live in the inner-cities.
>
> (Reiner, 1992; 763)

In public order policing like the G20 real-world policing example, this illustrates that the masculine, white model described by Silvestri (2017) is very clearly still deployed in relation to all members of the community. The example from the 23 policewomen data can be seen in the act of copying and cutting a policewoman's head off a photo from her desk drawer and superimposing it onto a picture of a grossly overweight woman anonymously and drip-feeding copies of this to her before the policewoman traced the culprit via fingerprints, to find it was her male colleague who used to sit opposite her (Cunningham and Ramshaw, 2020), illustrating that masculine hegemony remains intact, even if there is the potential for massive change from reform agendas. The Equal Opportunity and Human Rights approach to reviewing policing in Victoria is making attempts to challenge and punish these types of behaviours and other workplace harms in order to break these cultural norms and send a clear signal about them to all police officers. As the *Review of Policing* explained,

> This has not just affected individual women. It has reinforced a rigid, hypermasculine policing identity and caused cumulative harm to men and women who have witnessed the culture and shut off parts of themselves to adapt to it. It has also affected the way in which people police.
>
> (VEOHRC, Phase 3, 2019: 5)

The Review suggested a transformative approach to change policing culture and practice.

While the ideas about a specific character and nature of women have been discredited over time, ideas associated with these views have still been seen to be articulated and applied in the case of policewomen. As Woodeson (1993: 205) explained, equality was not a panacea in policing but a paradox, and women's experiences were mixed. Feminisms and feminist criminology, as we have seen, still have the ability to highlight women's experiences of policing, while women have faced sexist attitudes, harassment, and discrimination, and this allows exploration of the ways that women have been able to navigate these within their own journey of policing practice. The works of Brown and Heidensohn (2000) as well as Westmarland (2001) and Silvestri (2018) are important in providing some feminist criminology and policing insights along with others. In the case of the empirical research in relation to the 23 policewomen's experiences of policing, this feminist lens will be vital in uncovering and illustrating the same arguments about whether women officers are as good as their male colleagues and can do the same job, and we will examine some suggestions that *as* women they bring something different to the role of police officer, which is detailed in depth in Chapter 3. Next, I will explore an international example of an attempt at changing the male culture of policing more recently in Australia, which will be the focus of the next part of this chapter.

Review of Policing in Victoria, Australia

To suggest that policing in England still involves levels of bullying, harassment, and sex discrimination, as our 2020 findings clearly showed with all but three of the 23 officers feeling that they had experienced these things, should not be the end of the story with that data (Cunningham and Ramshaw, 2020). Moving forwards from the findings of that earlier study it is important to explore the direction in which policing can move from this place in order to prevent workplace harms, to enable promotion for all, and to begin attempts at real structural and cultural changes to provide transformation in policing. In this way an exploration of the situation in Australia will be important to our discussion of women officers, as similar issues can be seen within the studies and the response to these. The Equal Opportunities and Human Rights Commission working with the *Review of Policing* (2015) explored the culture within policing and found that barriers for women officers included issues like care responsibilities for policewomen, flexible working, and stigma which went alongside requests for this. The gender pay gap and pensions were also issues of note as well as bullying and fears of victimisation if these were reported, and it importantly included an expected backlash against measures and accountability for those who were causing these harms (VEOHRC, Phase 3, 2019: 2–3). Together, this review looks like a robust attempt to address the inequalities and culture of the male ideal in policing.

Shifting again from the theoretical to a practical sense, the Victorian Equal Opportunity and Human Rights Commission and the Victoria Police have worked together towards effecting transformational change as discussed and recommended by Squires (2003; 2007), Pateman (1988), and Scott (1988) regarding gender equality in policing. They began this transformation after asking questions about gendered violence and about women's safety in the workplace (VEOHRC, Phase 3, 2019). They saw domestic violence and abuse as being clearly linked to gender inequality, and with this as the root of problems such as sexual harassment, the wage gap, and pension inequalities, they suggested that not until this gendered approach was taken could these things begin to be discussed and resolved. The answer actually involves a feminist theoretical approach and review of policing, though the report does not use the still contentious 'f' word except in terms of one officer suggesting she is called 'the feminist', and that people go quiet when she enters the room, and feminism is only used in that whole document within the bibliography (VEOHRC, Phase 3, 2019). hooks's view that feminism remains unappealing appears again to be confirmed in the avoidance of using this word throughout the Report. This gendered perspective terminology

Re-emerging arguments 43

does fit well with ideas and definitions of feminism within this book, as discussed in Chapter 1, and with the aims of Wollstonecraft and with her arguments for human rights and equality and the sameness of women with men in terms of their human rights and rationality. Added to arguments which were put forward by Wollstonecraft, however, is the knowledge that difference should not be used to limit women's opportunities in terms of care roles and requirements for some flexibility. That the report also noted the outdated notions of woman and man which we have travelled and traced throughout this book is also worth noting. In 2021, these notions about what we are and what we can do still informs ideas about women and their nature, hundreds of years after Wollstonecraft flagged these arguments up and sought to change this. That the investigation in Victoria explored the nature, prevalence, drivers, and impact of sex discrimination, inequality, and gendered abuse of power which, while all explored in Wollstonecraft's works, can still be seen in relation to women and policing today is striking.

> Over the course of the five years of investigation, the team spent hours in conversation with women who had been sidelined, denigrated, and disrespected in the workplace. They explained that these officers had been denied promotions, access to development training, been the subject of sexist jokes, been humiliated, and at times been physically assaulted. This culture was found to have negatively impacted on female officers and harmed all officers who had seen and reacted to this in their policing style, according to the report. They made 20 recommendations to build transformative change. Challenging and changing this hypermasculinity in policing meant examining structures and systems, attitudes, and biases, and would require leadership and accountability, a compassionate and transparent response to workplace harm, redress for past wrongs and the development of a more respectful and inclusive culture that would allow both men and women to thrive.
>
> (VEOHRC, Phase 3, 2019: 5)

Importantly, they expected resistance and backlash, and sought to put measures in place for dealing with these. This should be an expected reaction to trying to transform a dominant and masculine police culture, and has been seen throughout the integration of women in policing with the threat against male privilege within such a patriarchal institution (Heidensohn 2002; 2012, Yoder, 1991). This report suggests that the review and transformative change will take years, and they suggest that gender equality should be achieved by 2030 (VEOHRC,

44 *Re-emerging arguments*

Phase 3, 2019: 6). They also suggest that legislative change is required, including a strengthening of the Equal Opportunity Act (2010), however is a missed opportunity in making feminist- informed change explicit. This third review adds a further 16 recommendations,

> This final review provides us a roadmap to achieve gender equality by 2030. It recognises that the changes we have made so far need to be embedded within our systems and structures and that we still have much work to do to shift behaviours and attitudes that lead to workplace harm.
>
> (VEOHRC, Phase 3, 2019: 8)

This approach to attempting transformational change is important in that it was an approach whereby the culture of policing within this area of Victoria, Australia, was put under a microscope by the Equal Opportunity and Human Rights Commission, which had provided a damning critique of how bad things were, but that was an external organisation which sought to work with policing to effect the change that was seen as necessary for policing. This external relationship was important in sending a clear message to all officers about the need to change and challenge this culture along with the expectation of backlash, at least initially.

Wollstonecraft's dilemma

The work from Squires (2003; 2007) provides further insight into the dilemma about sameness and difference which may help in understanding this issue for feminists. In discussions about the problems with the approach Wollstonecraft took, Squires (2003) considered contemporary debates about equality and diversity. She cited Pateman (1995) and her idea of Wollstonecraft's dilemma that equality and difference are antagonistic aims (Squires, 2003: 12). She explained that this debate was between liberal egalitarians and advocates of a politics of recognition. She argued that those from the equality perspective considered gender politically irrelevant, whereas difference theorists accepted and even celebrated gender differences (Squires, 2003: 13). She explained that the fundamental disagreement between these two sides centred on the question of impartiality – as an ideal of impartiality and an ideal of partiality respectively (Squires, 2003: 14). Squires suggested that 'Recognition of the negative effects of this dilemma upon feminist theory and practice has motivated many to attempt to negotiate a path beyond the dichotomy and to map out a third perspective – that of diversity' (Squires, 2003: 14).

Re-emerging arguments   45

She suggests that this approach is transformative rather than integrative, which just added women, or with difference theorists placing women at the centre this approach sought to deconstruct the centre. Squires argued that this represented 'the emergence of a new perspective that takes the deconstruction of binary oppositions to be its central task' (Squires, 2003: 15). This is in a similar vein to Scott's earlier (1988: 48) attempt at resolving the sameness and difference dilemma where she suggested the need for 'an equality that rests on differences' which disrupts the fixed binary opposition. A positive development in challenging this problematic dichotomy between equality and difference may be, according to Squires, 'mainstreaming' which moves beyond, but complements, equal treatment and positive action. She argued that

> Mainstreaming takes us beyond the classic opposition between equality of opportunity and equality of outcome, as embodied in equal treatment and positive action, by focusing on the structural reproduction of gender inequality and aiming to transform the policy process such that gender bias is eliminated.
>
> (Squires, 2003: 17)

Squires went on to argue that this mainstreaming should not be limited to gender as it could also address other inequalities, and noted one fear of this replacing rather than complementing the other two strategies (Squires, 2003: 22). She suggested that for some this would be more palatable than positive action strategies (Squires, 2003: 27). Squires's work on women and citizenship illustrates that well into the twenty-first century, reconciliation of the problems of calling for equality or difference have remained. The arguments about sameness and difference have also been explored from Scott's (1988) work to discussions about the sameness being used by Chávez, Nair, and Conrad (2015: 273) to examine the use of these arguments in relation to the Equal Rights Amendment in America. The problems relating to sameness and 'equality' for minorities is explored,

> In spite of Scott's powerful argument, this dichotomizing of equality and difference not only hindered ERA advocates in the 1970s but it also continues to constrain several struggles for so-called equality today. In our work as a collective, we see this struggle most starkly in debates surrounding 'marriage equality', where rhetorical and visual narratives of sameness saturate pro-gay-marriage political campaigns.1 'Sameness' in this case both makes a claim to normalcy and respectability that has been historically denied to sexual

46 *Re-emerging arguments*

minorities but also levels a demand that the state recognize only gay and lesbian kinship structures that mimic the ideology of family already upheld by contemporary marriage law: family units headed by monogamous conjugal couples. Here, difference is once again sacrificed in the clamouring toward equality, while ignoring much greater need for comprehensive family law reform.

(Chávez, Nair, and Conrad, 2015: 273)

Wollstonecraft argued in terms of equality, to avoid the claims of difference within the eighteenth century, whereas women in the nineteenth century used conceptions of woman as different in order to gain access and a specific role within policing, as we saw in Chapter 1. The arguments around impartiality and partiality remain, although Squires recommends a transformative approach with mainstreaming, which should complement both the equality and difference claims and help resolve the dilemma. The work by Squires (2003) on transformative politics illustrates that into the twenty-first century the gap between arguing for sameness or difference has remained an enduring issue for current feminists looking for resolution in mainstreaming. Squires (2007) does also warn that the potential of mainstreaming has yet to be achieved, suggesting a gap between the theory and practical limitations (Squires, 2007: 154). An equality and human rights approach alongside a recognition of difference, which is supported, should help negotiate the dichotomy towards inclusion and diversity. The support for difference may be in attitudinal terms or in structural terms providing flexible working patterns, for instance, which have traditionally included stigma and questions about commitment to the job, especially within policing. Extensive working-from-home policies and challenges have been met during the COVID-19 pandemic, and such practices may well extend after this time and may help. These structural and attitudinal changes should allow policewomen the opportunity to actualise that equality, in theory. While this review of Victorian policing in Australia aims towards shifting the gender inequality at play in current policing practice to effect change which will transform policing, the evidence for their success has not backed this up as yet. As Squires (2007) suggested, there is still a gap. Crenshaw's (1989; 2017) ideas remain insightful in relation to policing,

> It is somewhat ironic that those concerned with alleviating the ills of racism and sexism should adopt such a top-down approach to discrimination. If their efforts instead began with addressing the

Re-emerging arguments   47

needs and problems of those who are most disadvantaged and with restructuring and remaking the world where necessary, then others who are singularly disadvantaged would also benefit. In addition, it seems that placing those who currently are marginalized in the center is the most effective way to resist efforts to compartmentalize experiences and undermine potential collective action.

(Crenshaw, 1989: 167)

One example of the continuing gap between theory and practice in relation to dealing with sex discrimination can still be seen in the following real-world example. A police officer in Victoria, Australia, has been reinstated to his post after joking about grooming girls, upskirting, and talking to colleagues about giving a fake apology, and this is after the review of policing culture (Bucci, 2020). The police constable was said to be experiencing deteriorating mental health following the death of his mother, a dementia diagnosis of his father, and his suffering the birth of a stillborn child. This officer had been said to often use the word 'cunt' at work too, but this was not serious enough to be disciplined for. This officer's behaviour towards and about women in the 11 charges illustrates the practical problems in dealing with sexual harassment at work, and the news story also highlights the problem of these offences only coming to light in the public arena when they are appealed against. The news report in *The Guardian* goes on to disclose that

Cases heard by the board in the past five years include a senior sergeant who behaved 'disgracefully' towards a female police public servant, including exposing his penis to her, a sergeant who had or sought relationships with four junior staff, and another sergeant who made inappropriate comments while briefing colleagues about the VEOHRC review.

In several cases, police found to have sexually harassed colleagues also behaved inappropriately against other women, including breaching court orders against former partners or using police databases to find personal information about women who they wanted to pursue sexual relationships with.

Multiple officers were dismissed for having sexual relationships with women they had met because they were victims of family violence who had sought the help of police.

(Bucci, 2020, Victoria police officer dismissed for sexual harassment reinstated | Australian police and policing | *The Guardian*)

48 *Re-emerging arguments*

These offence types are of interest as they clearly illustrate misogyny in practice in relation to the offences committed by policemen, which are informed by abuse of male privilege and power. The ways in which such offences are met and dealt with sends an important signal to all other officers and are obviously important for society in general. These offences will be especially important to come back to in relation to the next chapter. In Chapter 3 we will examine a quantitative survey about the sameness or difference of women and male officers who have been disciplined across three force areas in England and Wales over a five-year period, to explore whether this can add further insight into the difference and sameness debate and where policing may go in the future.

Summary

This chapter has continued to trace the ideas and discussion of the sameness and difference of policewomen and policemen, seeing Wollstonecraft's ideas in policing debates into the 1990s and beyond. I returned to the policewomen data, given these ideas about the sameness and difference of officers, which adds another layer of analysis to the data, and which may be useful in re-exploring data about policewomen's identity and how they negotiate this within their policing role. Wollstonecraft's dilemma is further examined and resolution appeared to be considered in relation to transformational change, such as that suggested by the investigation into policing in Victoria, Australia. The report's approach was seen to adopt a rigorous feminist critique of policing, without using the 'f' word, from an agency outside of policing, which was useful, and that had expected a backlash to the measures suggested, and included ideas for further work regarding these attitudes. Disturbingly, however, the real-world example illustrated the undeniable gap which remains between theory and practice in relation to this transformational change, as seen in Bucci's newspaper report (2020).

3 Feminist use of Freedom of Information requests (FOI)

This chapter explores suggestions that *as* women, policewomen bring something different to policing. Here I examine the re-emergence of the difference debate about the nature of woman and some outdated ideas about women and men, as well as exploring different styles of policing practice which have been found within other studies especially in relation to women officers and better citizen-encounter styles. The work from Rabe-Hemp (2008a) as well as that more recently from Barnes, Beaulieu, and Saxton (2017) and Roman (2020) will help illuminate and inform these debates. I will move on from issues about women officers adding difference, which were the initial arguments used for women's early integration into policing, to explore some disciplinary data of policewomen and policemen, to see if this can add any insight into police behaviours and to consider any marked differences that emerge, and what these may mean.

Policing, not just in England and Wales where we are used to policing by consent, relies on citizens' views of its representation in relation to its legitimacy (Skolnick, 2008). Brown and Silvestri (2019) have also highlighted that different force areas are different in relation to their openness to progressive change in terms of police culture, while others remain resistant to change, which may be worth keeping in mind when looking at the results of the three police areas. Trust in the police allows citizens to provide evidence for cases, which is vital in the pursuit of justice, as well as allowing those who have been victimised to seek help and justice. Examples of police corruption, and a lack of trust in the police which follows these examples raises questions about the legitimacy of policing and justice for different communities. Barnes, Beaulieu, and Saxton (2017) argue that 'Police departments around the world need to improve their image to regain the public's trust. In this article we considered one policy that might be effective at restoring trust in the police: adding women to the force' (Barnes, Beaulieu, and Saxton,

DOI: 10.4324/9781003149156-4

50 *Feminist use of Freedom of Information*

2017:13). They note the use of this method of increasing the numbers of women police within some countries such as Brazil and Mexico to reduce corruption and help restore the legitimacy of policing (Barnes, Beaulieu and Saxton, 2017). They also provide examples where this approach has helped build trust between citizens and the police, such as with female traffic police in Petaling Jaya in Kuala Lumpur, Malaysia, with some success. In their study they argue that there are potentially three factors which may account for the perception that women officers are more effective at combating corruption which are,

> gender stereotypes that women are more ethical and honest, perceptions of women officers as outsiders, and perceptions of women as more risk averse than men (Barnes and Beaulieu 2014, 2016).
>
> (Barnes, Beaulieu, and Saxton, 2017: 1)

They explain the levels of the problems about the image of policing in America as being at about 30 per cent of citizens who thought the police were doing an excellent or a good job (Barnes, Beaulieu and Saxton, 2017), and this was before the death of George Floyd and the #Blacklivesmatter movement which has brought police brutality and racially motivated violence to the eyes of the world (Day, 2019). Barnes, Beaulieu, and Saxton suggest that women are perceived to be more ethical as an after-effect of the gender stereotypes which depict women as more honest, compassionate, and concerned with people's welfare. While their study did not find support for this factor of women actually being more ethical and honest, it did find support for the other two – that they were outsiders and therefore less likely to be involved with corruption and criminal networks, and that their behaviour is more risk averse (Barnes, Beaulieu, and Saxton, 2017: 9). They go on to suggest that 'Learning more about the specific stereotypes that underlie perceptions of women is important for thinking about the role of women in public service and government' (Barnes, Beaulieu, and Saxton, 2017: 13). In a similar vein, Rabe-Hemp (2008a) suggested that her research examined a different style of policing that women officers were engaged in which 'suggests that women are much less likely than men to utilize extreme controlling behaviour, such as threats, physical restraint, search and arrest' (Rabe-Hemp, 2008a: 426). While Rabe-Hemp (2008a) acknowledged that assumptions about feminine traits in policing tasks is an oversimplification of conceptualising the meaning of the impact of gender in policing, importantly she recognised that

> Female officers struggle to integrate into the police subculture and limited adoption of the resultant us vs them attitude may explain

Feminist use of Freedom of Information 51

female officers astonishingly low rates of police force and misconduct and have important implications for police accountability.

(Rabe-Hemp, 2008b: 265–6)

This suggestion of policewomen's low rates of misconduct will be
further explored in the next section of this chapter; however, the
implications will be important if this is the case in helping raise confidence and legitimacy in policing. After exploring women's experiences
of undertaking policing across four decades and reviewing rich qualita-
tive data in Chapter 2, this chapter continues examining the questions
about women police officers and their behaviours. Here I will use an
innovative quantitative research method of exploring disciplinary data
of male and female officers across three force areas over a five-year
period. This Freedom of Information (FOI) data will allow a window
into seeing the types of disciplinary breaches made by police officers
and allow us to question whether there are major differences and similarities between them in terms of the numbers and gendered breakdown
within these patterns. The question surrounding whether women officers
are as good as their male colleagues and can do the same job as well has
been on the policing research agenda for many years and crosses many
national borders, as seen in Chapter 2 with the Victorian Police working
with Equal Opportunities and Human Rights Commission to effect a
policing culture change in Australia (VEOHRC, Phase 3, 2019).

This disciplinary study is quite a departure from research which has
tended to focus on the police-citizen interaction and gendered behaviour
of officers (Rabe-Hemp, 2008a; Barnes, Beaulieu, and Saxton, 2017), or
on citizen perceptions of aggression from male and female officers in
uniform (Simpson and Croft, 2020) to focus on their own disciplinary
offences and their relation to the main question this book is concerned
with, that is, conceptions about how the 'nature' of woman which still
inform policing practice. Of special pertinence is the suggestion that
policewomen are more moral and maternal than policemen, which
was the argument used for their initial inclusion in policing, seen in
Chapter 1, and the stereotype from this conception that they are more
ethical remains, according to Barnes, Beaulieu, and Saxton (2017).
Novak, Brown, and Frank's (2011) US study concentrates on female
and male officer difference in arrest behaviour, while Barnes, Beaulieu,
and Saxton (2017) explore issues of trust and legitimacy in policing and
citizen interaction as well as how this may be improved with the
employment of female officers. Rabe-Hemp (2008a) studied officer–
citizen dynamics and found that 'Female officers' underutilization of
force may actually produce police-citizen encounters that are safer for
female officers and the citizens they encounter' (Rabe-Hemp, 2008a:

52 *Feminist use of Freedom of Information*

431). These studies also differ from the US study of policewomen and crime by Stinson, Todak, and Dodge (2013), who explored this subject via a Google news and Google Alerts media data collection approach. They found a difference in the misdeeds and offences between policewomen and policemen, with women involved in profit-related crime as opposed to sexual or violent and sexual violence crime. Policemen were seen to have been involved in these offence types in Victoria, Australia, too (Bucci, 2020). Simpson and Croft's (2020) study employed a novel data collection approach using Amazon's Mechanical Turk, or MTurk (Simpson and Croft, 2020: 6), to explore the effects of officer gender on citizens' perceptions of officer aggression. They went on to find that perceptions of female aggression were low when the officers were wearing civilian clothes; however, it was perceived as similarly aggressive when they were wearing a uniform. This chapter will explore the FOI data, which provides another facet of information we have available to us about police officers, offering a new and different perspective with which to explore how male police officers and female police officers behave in terms of how they engage with disciplinary offences.

While misogyny appears to be amplified within police culture, it can be seen intensified at the intersections of gender, class, and race. Cressida Dick was 'disgusted' that pictures and selfies together with murdered black women in London were taken and shared by her officers, while Mrs Smallman, the mother of the women, was critical of the police response and the lack of searching for her missing daughters and was rightly horrified to learn of the pictures taken (Bashir, 2020). She revealed to the BBC that the lack of police response was due to her daughters being black women from a council estate. While the officers were arrested for misconduct and investigated by the Independent Office for Police Conduct (IOPC), this real-world example in England and Wales clearly illustrates a misogynistic police culture and how a feminist intersectional analysis would be appropriate in exploring disciplinary records of the police. Responding to examples such as these is vital in building trust that is required for policing to work for citizens, and for justice for all victims of crime. It also sends a clear message to police officers. Unfortunately, this is not the only such example, which is a continuing cause for concern (Townsend and Jayanetti, 2021).

New 'woman as different' arguments

In recent times we see the re-emergence of the nature of woman as different arguments, which suggest women officers add something extra to the way they perform the role of policing. From America, Roman

Feminist use of Freedom of Information 53

(2020) recently argued that, even though research appears to find benefits brought by women to policing, the figures seem to be stuck at the 12 per cent level for women police officers in America.

Women are consistently rated as trusted by their communities and, importantly, are motivated to serve communities in an era of decreased police legitimacy. Women have high levels of interpersonal communication skills, which translates into more effective practices in the field. Women are found to have a calming effect on male partners in high-stress and dangerous assignments, resulting in fewer police deaths. Higher levels of female representation are associated with organizations that emphasize community policing. Female police officers have a positive influence on the perceived job performance, trustworthiness, and fairness of a police agency, perhaps increasing the public's willingness to cooperate in the production of positive public safety outcomes. Female officers are less likely to use force, use excessive force, or be named in a lawsuit than male officers. Research has found that male officers were more likely than female officers to be aggressive as a result of some quality of the encountered member of the public, such as race or socioeconomic class. Even though studies show that subjects use the same amount of force against female officers as against male officers, and in some cases, more force, female officers are more successful in defusing violent or aggressive behavior.

(Roman, 2020, Police chief online)

Methodology

This chapter has the major focus of an empirical study with data derived from three force areas over a period of years (2007–12) from two city police services, and one large town in England, which were chosen because I had some knowledge of the three, had built up contacts, and knew officers within these three force areas. This chapter seeks to add a new dimension to the debate about female and male officers by exploring their disciplinary records over a period of time, to see whether they engage in the same types of disciplinary offence, do this in the same numbers, or whether there are discernible differences, and discussing what this may mean. This distinctive study is a window into policing, representation, and culture and will be an insightful, if not well-used feminist research method (Bows, 2017). Bows (2017) suggests FOI requests could be used much more often to uncover information which can be opened up for further scrutiny. Policing, like most organisations,

54 *Feminist use of Freedom of Information*

requires this kind of scrutiny from outside of the institution for independent transparency and impartiality. Importantly, this chapter adds a picture of male and female police officer behaviour within the given timeframe and provides insight into policewomen's, disciplinary offences in relation to policemen's offences with far-reaching implications in relation to policing practice and community trust. This research method of data collection, however, has advantages over other methods as it is in the public realm if it is asked for, and if it is deemed to be in the public interest, the data is then disclosed. Writing this book during the COVID-19 pandemic and lockdown also highlights how this could be a safe research method to be undertaken during periods of pandemic and limits on travel. There are some concerning real-world examples in England and Wales which illustrate current issues regarding police culture and discipline and how this may impact on different communities which support studies such as this. As seen in Chapter 2, sexual harassment and blocked opportunities were found with the 23 policewomen, and misogyny was seen with offences such as domestic violence, which were also noted in relation to police culture and masculine hegemony in the *Review of Policing* in Australia, and this also arises in one of the disciplinary records in this study (VEOHRC, Phase 3, 2019). The importance of transparency and policing by consent in this country were noted in relation to the stopping and searching of Black athletes in London recently alongside news that the officers were disciplined for the way they approached this (Dodd, 2020). This window into the numbers of police officer staff broken down into men and women and classified into the kinds of disciplinary offences they were involved in is an interesting study on gender and behaviour. One of the strongest arguments for undertaking this study is that it may provide some insight into the arguments which we have seen from the past in Chapter 1 and also insight regarding women's nature, initially used to allow women's inclusion in policing, as discussed in Chapter 2. Arguments such as women being more moral than men, behaving differently, and being more trustworthy and less confrontational appear to resurface, or continue, as does the continuance of toxic masculinity and misogynistic examples within policing.

Limitations of this FOI study

There are a number of issues to note in relation to problems surrounding this type of data collection. One major limitation is the lack of knowledge about ethnicity and sexuality in relation to the officers who were disciplined. This limits the conclusions made and warrants much

Feminist use of Freedom of Information 55

further and more detailed research to be undertaken in the future. Another problem is that this study only includes those officers caught undertaking misdeeds which I need to acknowledge and take account of. This study therefore is limited to those officers who are reported and caught, where the charge is upheld and they are disciplined, which will exclude behaviours seen as 'banter' and 'horseplay', which have been noted in most studies of women's lived experiences of policing. Procedural problems also include the errors and typos in the data sent out from police service areas for analysis, and this data did include a few typos, which are highlighted. There is also the problem of knowing the type of misdeed but not knowing the detail or context of this in relation to having a deeper understanding, which did also emerge. The way that discipline is categorised and dealt with by the police changes often and therefore becomes problematic to compare. Changes from pre- to New Taylor discipline rules as noted by the police in the data they provided within the time frame of this study had an impact in that it makes it very difficult to produce clear comparisons over time, as these have changed every couple of years, so you are never comparing like with like (IOPC, 2020). While using the FOI approach to data collection has its problems, especially for a social scientist more used to gaining rich individual data from policewomen's own lived experiences (Cunningham and Ramshaw, 2020), it is useful in illustrating the extent of female and male involvement in disciplinary proceedings within the police, so that as a feminist researcher I can explore what these numbers may mean. I was fortunate to receive advice regarding illustrating the data from my friend and colleague Dr Alison Jarvis, who has had much more experience working with quantitative data than I have, and was generous with her time. Notwithstanding all of these limitations faced, the data will provide an important insight into police officer behaviour which we would not have otherwise, and that adds insight to gendered police behaviour.

These issues such as police ethics and proportionate police practice remain resonant when exploring a real-world example in 2020 where we see five officers stopping and searching athlete Bianca Williams and her partner in London, using handcuffs on them while their baby son was in the car, and making a Merlin report regarding the child. The IOPC investigated this regarding the officers' misconduct, use of force, and the suggestion of racial profiling (Dodd, 2020). It is exactly this kind of example which illustrates why it is important for the police service areas to be open and transparent about officer disciplinary reports and details to the citizens they serve. This kind of example severely erodes public confidence in policing, especially in BAME communities, and

56 Feminist use of Freedom of Information

therefore this will impact on faith and belief in policing and justice in England and Wales, so there is a lot at stake. It serves also to illustrate that Reiner's ideas (1992) about those at the sharp end of police practice have not changed very much in the intervening decades. We will also need to remain mindful that policing has historically been a white male preserve, which is active and aggressive, and that policing culture has a part to play in terms of behaviour within the workplace and safety issues for female officers which have been seen to have occurred in terms of sexual harassment, 'banter', and blocked opportunities (Cunningham and Ramshaw, 2020). The change in discipline regulations means that the figures that follow are illustrative rather than definitive within the 'Service', 'Constabulary', and 'Force' Police areas.

Service police area

Service Table 3.1 (below) shows that policemen are proportionately more likely to have faced disciplinary action than policewomen. During this period, the proportion of women officers nationally ranged between 23 per cent and 28 per cent, but the proportion tended to be lower within Service police. At best, this would suggest a 5:1 ratio between men and women. In fact, year on year until 2010, men outnumbered women in most allegations by a greater ratio. The only instances for women being potentially disproportionately represented were for management action in 2008 and 2011; and for formal action in 2012.

The numbers in Service Table 3.1 below clearly show more male officers facing disciplinary action at 2,654 total offences in comparison with

Service Table 3.1 Police officers facing disciplinary action by gender 2006–12

Action taken	2006		2007		2008		2009		2010		2011		2012		Total	
	F	M	F	M	F	M	F	M	F	M	F	M	F	M	F	M
Fast Track		1		2		1										4
Formal Action						21	**35**	**275**	45	**315**	**41**	**237**	3	11	124	859
Formal Discipline		10														10
Formal Misconduct	**10**	73	**1**	92	6	**68**	1	5							18	238
Management Action					3	9	37	199	24	101	12	52	1	7	77	368
Written Warning	58	408	56	369	64	362	2	33		1		2			180	1175
Total	**68**	**492**	**57**	**463**	**73**	**461**	**75**	**512**	**69**	**417**	**53**	**291**	**4**	**18**	**399**	**2654**

Feminist use of Freedom of Information 57

Service Table 3.2 Nature of breaches by gender 2006–08

Year >	2006		2007		2008		Totals		
	M	F	M	F	M	F	M	F	All
Nature of breach									
Honesty and integrity	4	1	7		4		15	1	**16**
Politeness and tolerance	3		3		5		11	0	**11**
Not following lawful orders	11		12		14		37	0	**37**
Use of force/abuse of authority	**3**		**5**		**6**		**14**	**0**	**14**
Performance of duties	11	1	29		6	1	46	2	**48**
General conduct	18	1	15	1	20	1	53	3	**56**
Confidentiality		1			1		1	1	**2**
Criminal offences	23	6	21		12	4	56	10	**66**
Totals	**73**	**10**	**92**	**1**	**70**	**6**	**233**	**17**	**250**

female officers at 399 total offences during this period. Service Table 3.2 above illustrates the nature of the offence in 'Service', which indicates a marked difference in the use of force across all years in terms of gender and also illustrates the reality in relation to women who are involved in some honesty offences in contrast to the stereotype where they are seen as more honest, as found by Barnes, Beaulieu, and Saxton (2017).

A comparison of Service Tables 3.5 and 3.6 reveals that, again, there is an overall under-representation of women in most categories, though with some exceptions. Women were over-represented amongst those facing no action in all three years; over-represented for management advice in 2010; and over-represented for dismissals in 2011.

Service Table 3.7 on page 62, is the clearest indication of the types of different disciplinary behaviours engaged in by male and female officers.

Service 2006–09

For male officers during the period 2006–09, criminal offences were 23 in 2006, 21 in 2007, 12 in 2008, and none in 2009. In terms of general conduct, 18 policemen breached this in 2006, 15 in 2007, 20 in 2008, and 5 in 2009. Performance of duties saw 11 breaches in 2006, 29 in 2007, 6 in 2008, and none in 2009, whereas politeness and tolerance saw 3 breaches in 2006, 3 in 2007, 5 in 2008, and none in 2009. Breaches of lawful orders were 11 in 2006, 12 in 2007, 14 in 2008, and none in 2009. Honesty and integrity saw 4 breaches in 2006, 7 in 2007, 4 in 2008, and none in 2009. Use of force and abuse of authority saw 3 breaches in 2006, 5 in 2007, 6 in 2008, and none in 2009, while confidentiality

Service Table 3.3 Results of allegations of formal misconduct by Service Police (females; 2006–08)

Nature of breach	2006					2007					2008					Totals					All outcomes
	Dismissal	Required to resign	Fine	Reprimand	No action	Dismissal	Required to resign	Fine	Reprimand	No action	Dismissal	Required to resign	Fine	Reprimand	No action	Dismissal	Required to resign	Fine	Reprimand	No action	
Honesty and integrity		1															1				**1**
Politeness and tolerance																					
Not following lawful orders																					
Force/abuse of authority																					
Performance of duties		1									1					1	1				**2**
General conduct		1						1				1					1	2			**3**
Confidentiality	1															1					**1**
Criminal offences	1	3	1	1										4		1	3	1	5		**10**
Totals	**2**	**6**	**1**	**1**				**1**			**1**	**1**		**4**		**3**	**7**	**2**	**5**		**17**

Service Table 3.4 Results of allegations of formal misconduct by Service Police (males; 2006–08)

Nature of breach	2006						2007						2008						Totals						All outcomes
	Dismissal	Required to resign	Reduction in rank	Fine	Reprimand/Caution	No action	Dismissal	Required to resign	Reduction in rank	Fine	Reprimand/Caution Reprimand	No action	Dismissal	Required to resign	Reduction in rank	Fine	Reprimand/Caution Reprimand	No action	Dismissal	Required to resign	Reduction in rank	Fine	Reprimand/Caution Reprimand	No action	
Honesty and integrity	2	2					1	5			1		4						7	7	0	0	1	0	**15**
Politeness and tolerance	1		1	1				1		1	1		2			2	1		3	1	1	4	2	0	**11**
Fail to follow lawful orders	3	1		2	5			2			5		3	1	7	5	3		6	4	7	7	13	0	**37**
Force/abuse of authority		1		2				3				2	3				2	1	3	4	0	2	2	3	**14**
Performance of duties		1		5	5			3		16	10		2		1	3			2	4	1	24	15	0	**46**
General conduct	2	3		11	2		1	4		6	4		2	4			4	10	5	11	0	21	16	0	**53**
Confidentiality									1										0	0	1	0	0	0	**1**
Criminal offences		6	1	9	5	2	3	4	1	7	6		3	3		2	4		6	13	2	18	15	2	**56**
Totals	**8**	**14**	**2**	**30**	**17**	**2**	**5**	**23**	**1**	**30**	**27**	**2**	**19**	**8**	**8**	**16**	**20**	**1**	**32**	**44**	**12**	**76**	**54**	**5**	**233**

Service Table 3.5 Results of formal action by Service Police (females; 2009–11)

Year >	2009				2010				2011				Totals				
Nature of breach	Dismissal	Written warning	Management advice	No action	Dismissal	Written warning	Management advice	No action	Dismissal	Written warning	Management advice	No action	Dismissal	Written warning	Management advice	No action	All outcomes
Honesty and integrity	4	2			2	2	1		1				7	4	1	0	**12**
Authority, respect, courtesy		1		2		1	1			5	3		0	7	4	2	**13**
Equality and diversity		1											0	1	0	0	**1**
Use of force					1								0	1	0	0	**1**
Orders and instructions		2				7	2			5	2		0	14	4	0	**18**
Duties and responsibilities		13	2	2	1	8	6	2	1	10	3		2	31	11	4	**48**
Confidentiality		1				3					2		0	4	2	0	**6**
Fitness for duty										1			0	1	0	0	**1**
Discreditable conduct		2	3		2	4	2		4	4			6	10	5	0	**21**
Totals	**4**	**22**	**5**	**4**	**5**	**26**	**12**	**2**	**6**	**25**	**10**	**0**	**15**	**73**	**27**	**6**	**121**

Service Table 3.6 Results of formal action by Service Police (males; 2009–11)

Year >	2009				2010				2011				Totals				
Nature of breach	Dismissal	Written warning	Management advice	No action	Dismissal	Written warning	Management advice	No action	Dismissal	Written warning	Management advice	No action	Dismissal	Written warning	Management advice	No action	All outcomes
Honesty and integrity	6	13	1	1	6	6	2	1	1	6		1	13	25	3	3	**44**
Authority, respect, courtesy		43	7	1	11	35	8	1	1	21	12		12	99	27	2	**140**
Equality and diversity					1	5				1	1		1	6	1	0	**8**
Use of force		5	2	1		5		4					0	10	2	5	**17**
Orders and instructions	2	24	6	2	2	32	12			31	14		4	87	32	2	**125**
Duties and responsibilities	4	45	11	3	6	64	16	3	1	54	21	2	11	163	48	8	**230**
Confidentiality		2				8	3		1	4			1	14	3	0	**18**
Fitness for duty		1				4				3			0	8	0	0	**8**
Discreditable conduct	24	62	6	1	29	37	7		16	21	8		69	120	21	1	**211**
Totals	**36**	**195**	**33**	**9**	**55**	**196**	**48**	**9**	**20**	**141**	**56**	**3**	**111**	**532**	**137**	**21**	**801**

62 Feminist use of Freedom of Information

Service Table 3.7 Misconduct and formal action: proportions by breach and by gender (2006–11)

Time frame >	2006–2008				Time frame >	2009–2011			
Nature of breach	% all male		% all female		Nature of breach	% all male		% all female	
Honesty and integrity	15	7%	1	6%	Honesty and integrity	41	6%	12	10%
% breach	94%		6%		% breach	77%		23%	
Politeness and tolerance	11	5%	0	0%	Authority, respect, courtesy	138	19%	11	10%
% breach	100%		0%		% breach	93%		7%	
Not following lawful orders	34	15%	0	0%	Orders and instructions	78	11%	18	16%
% breach	100%		0%		% breach	81%		19%	
Using force/ abusing authority	11	5%	0	0%	Use of force	12	2%	1	1%
% breach	100%		0%		% breach	92%		8%	
Performance of duties	46	20%	2	13%	Duties and responsibilities	222	30%	44	38%
% breach	96%		4%		% breach	83%		17%	
General conduct	53	24%	3	19%	Fitness for duty	8	1%	1	1%
% breach	95%		5%		% breach	89%		11%	
Confidentiality	1	0%	1	6%	Confidentiality	18	2%	6	5%
% breach	50%		50%		% breach	75%		25%	
Criminal offences	54	24%	9	56%	Discreditable conduct	210	29%	21	18%
% breach	86%		14%		% breach	91%		9%	
Totals	**225**		**16**		Equality and diversity	8	1%	1	1%
					% breach	89%		11%	
					Totals	**735**		**115**	

Note: Table figures exclude cases resulting in no action.

saw only one breach in 2008 over this period. In contrast, in relation to policewomen, in 2010 there were 69 policewoman breaches in contrast to 467 policeman breaches of the regulations. For the policewomen, there were 5 breaches for honesty and integrity, 2 for authority, respect, and courtesy, 1 for use of force, 9 for orders and instructions, 17 for duties and responsibilities, 3 for confidentiality, and 8 for discreditable conduct breaches. For the policemen, there were 15 for honesty and integrity, 55 for authority, respect and courtesy, 6 for equality and

Feminist use of Freedom of Information 63

diversity, 9 for use of force, 48 for orders and instructions, 89 for duties and responsibilities, 11 for confidentiality, 73 for discreditable conduct, and 5 awaiting.

Service 2011

In 2011, there were 53 policewomen and 338 policemen involved in breaching the regulations. For the policewomen, they were 1 for honesty and integrity, 8 for authority, respect, and courtesy, 7 for orders and instructions, 14 for duties and responsibilities, 2 confidentiality, 1 for fitness for duty, and 8 for discreditable conduct. For the policemen during this same period, there were 8 for honesty and integrity, 34 for authority, respect and courtesy, 2 for equality and diversity, 45 for orders and instructions, 78 for duties and responsibilities, 5 for confidentiality, 3 for fitness for duty, 45 for discreditable conduct, and 5 for challenge and reporting improper conduct.

Service 2012

Finally, in 2012 there were 3 female officer breaches as compared with 20 policemen breaching the regulations. Broken down into the types of breach by sex, the three female breaches were orders and instructions. The breaches by policemen were authority, respect, and courtesy 2, orders and instructions 2, duties and responsibilities 4, fitness for duty 1, and discreditable conduct 2.

Overall we see male disciplines decreasing from 733 in 2006 to 20 in 2012, and female numbers from 68 to 4 respectively.

Service 2011–12

We can see that 32 females were disciplined during 2011–12, broken down into 25 cases of formal action and 7 cases of management action taken. During this same period, 179 male officers were disciplined, with 147 receiving formal action, 30 management action, and 2 written warnings. For the data for 2012, formal action was taken with 3 female officers (down 38), with management action against 1 (See Service Table 3.8 on page 64), while formal action taken against 11 males, management action against 52, and 2 on written warnings. Sex and the type of offence were also provided for this data in Service Tables 3.8 and 3.9 below, which I separated into female and male, 2011/2012.

In terms of the type of breach policewomen were involved in with formal action, these included authority, respect, and courtesy (3), orders

64   *Feminist use of Freedom of Information*

Service Table 3.8 Formal action results and breaches female 2011–12

Officer Gender	Breach details	Management advice	Written warning	Awaiting	Grand total
Female	02 Authority, Respect and Courtesy	1	2		3
Female	05 Orders and Instructions	2	8		10
Female	06 Duties and Responsibilities	1	8		9
Female	07 Confidentiality	2			2
Female	08 Fitness for Duty		1		1
Female Total		6	19		25

Service Table 3.9 Formal action results and breaches male 2011–12

Officer Gender	Breach details	Management advice	Written warning	Awaiting	Grand Total
Male	01 Honesty and Integrity		4		4
Male	02 Authority, Respect and Courtesy	8	16		24
Male	03 Equality and Diversity	1			1
Male	05 Orders and Instructions	8	16		24
Male	06 Duties and Responsibilities	20	39		59
Male	07 Confidentiality		2		2
Male	08 Fitness for Duty		3		3
Male	09 Discreditable Conduct	7	11		18
Male	10 Challenging and Reporting Improper Conduct	1	4		5
Male	Awaiting			7	7
Male Total		45	95	7	147
Male and Female Total		**51**	**114**	**7**	**172**

and instructions (10), duties and responsibilities (9), confidentiality (2), and fitness for duty (1), making up the 25 cases.

During this same period and as detailed in Service Table 3.9 above, breaches resulting in formal action for the male officers included honesty

Feminist use of Freedom of Information 65

and integrity (4), authority, respect, and courtesy (24), equality and diversity (1), orders and instructions (24), duties and responsibilities (59), confidentiality (2), fitness for duty (3), discreditable conduct (18), challenging and reporting improper conduct (5), and awaiting formal action (7), making up the 147 total formal action cases of policemen.

Constabulary Police area

Constabulary Table 3.1 Alleged offences, type, male and female 2007–11

Year	Alleged offence	rank	m	f	Outcome
2007	Lawful orders/general conduct	PC	1		dismissal
	Abuse of authority/general conduct	PC	1		reprimand
	Performance of duties/lawful orders	PC	1		fined
2008	Misuse of electronic communications policy	PC	1		superintendent warning
	Neglect of duty	PC	1		
	Abuse of authority	PC	1		
	Politeness and tolerance	PC	1		
	Performance of duties	PC	1		
	Performance of duties	Sgt	1		
	Failure in duty	PC	4		
	Duties and responsibilities	PC		1	
	Duties and responsibilities	Sgt	1		
	Abuse of authority/general conduct	PC	1		
	Criminal conviction	PC/Sgt	2		caution
	Misuse of PNC, performance, gen conduct	PC	1		req. to resign; fined on appeal
2009	Performance of duties	Sgt	1		reduced in rank
	Performance of duties	PC	1		written warning
	Performance of duties	Sgt	1		management advice
	Performance of duties	PC	1		superintendent warning
	Performance of duties/general conduct	PC	1		dismissal
	Failure in duty	PC	1		superintendent warning
	Duties and responsibilities	Sgt	1		written warning
	Duties and responsibilities	PC	3	1	
	Duties and responsibilities	Sgt	1		management advice
	Misuse of electronic communications policy	PC	1		superintendent warning
	Discreditable conduct	PC	1		final written warning
	Discreditable conduct	PC	1		management advice
	Discreditable conduct	PC	4		written warning

(*continued*)

66 Feminist use of Freedom of Information

Constabulary Table 3.1 Cont.

Year	Alleged offence	rank	m	f	Outcome
2010	Duties and responsibilities	PC	1		written warning
	Duties and responsibilities	PC	3		management advice
	Duties and responsibilities	PC	1	1	
	Authority, respect and courtesy	PC	2		
	General conduct x 2; politeness & tolerance	PC	1		dismissal
	Misuse of electronic communications policy	PC	1		written warning
	Misuse of electronic communications policy	PC	1		management advice
	Orders and instructions	Insp	1		
	Discreditable conduct	PC	2		final written warning
	Honesty and integrity	PC	1		dismissal
2011	Misuse of police vehicle	PC	1		management advice
	Discreditable conduct	PC	1		dismissal
	Discreditable conduct	Insp	1		final written warning
	Discreditable conduct	Ch Insp	1		
		TOTALS	**54**	**3**	

Constabulary Table 3.2 Rank, offence, verdict and action 2007–11

Date	Rank of police officer	The alleged offence	Verdict of disciplinary proceedings	Disciplinary action
2007	Police constable male	Lawful orders/ general conduct	Guilty	Dismissed from service in May 2008
2007	PC Male	Abuse of authority/ general conduct	Guilty	Reprimand
2007	PC Male	Performance of duties/ lawful orders	Guilty	Fined

Date	Employee Type	Nature	Outcome of internal procedures	Comment
Feb 2008	PC Male	Misuse of the force electronic & communication policy	Superintendents Warning	
Mar 08	PC Male	Neglect of duty	Superintendents Warning	
Apr 08	PC Male	Abuse of authority	Superintendents Warning	

Feminist use of Freedom of Information 67

Constabulary Table 3.2 Cont.

Date	Employee Type	Nature	Outcome of internal procedures	Comment
May 08	PC Male	Politeness and Tolerance	Superintendents Warning	
May 08	PC Male	Performance of duties	Superintendents Warning	
May 08	PC Male	Failure in duty	Superintendents Warning	
May 08	PC Female	Duties and Responsibilities	Superintendents Warning	
Jul 08	PC Male	Failure in duty	Superintendents Warning	
Jul 08	PC Male	Failure in duty	Superintendents Warning	
Jul 08	PC Male	Abuse of authority and general conduct	Reprimand	Misconduct Hearing
Sep 08	Sergeant Male	Criminal Conviction	Caution	Misconduct Hearing
Sep 08	PC Male	Failure in duty	Superintendents Warning	
Sep 08	Sergeant Male	Duties and responsibilities	Superintendents Warning	
Nov 08	Sergeant Male	Performance of duties	Superintendents Warning	
Nov 08	PC Male	Criminal Conviction	Caution	Misconduct Hearing
Dec 08	PC Male	Misuse of PNC, Performance of duties and General conduct	Required to resign. Re-instated on appeal and fined.	Misconduct Hearing
Jan 09	Sergeant Male	Performance of Duties	Reduced in rank	Misconduct Hearing
Jan 09	PC Male	Performance of duties	Superintendents warning	
Feb 09	PC Male	Failure in duty	Superintendents warning	
Feb 09	PC Male	Discreditable conduct	Management advice	Misconduct meeting
Mar 09	PC Male	Misuse of the electronic communication policy	Superintendents warning	
Mar 09	PC Male	Discreditable conduct	Written warning	Misconduct meeting
Jun 09	PC Male	Duties and responsibilities	Written warning	Misconduct meeting

(*continued*)

68 *Feminist use of Freedom of Information*

Constabulary Table 3.2 Cont.

Date	Employee Type	Nature	Outcome of internal procedures	Comment
Jul 09	PC Male	Discreditable conduct	Written warning	Misconduct meeting
Jul 09	PC Male	Discreditable conduct	Written warning	Misconduct meeting
Jul 09	Sergeant Male	Duties and Responsibilities	Written warning	Misconduct meeting
Jul 09	PC Male	Duties and Responsibilities	Written warning	Misconduct meeting
Jul 09	PC Male	Duties and Responsibilities	Written warning	Misconduct meeting
Jul 09	PC Female	Duties and Responsibilities	Written warning	Misconduct meeting
Jul 09	PC Male	Duties and Responsibilities	Written warning	Misconduct meeting
Aug 09	PC Male	Performance of duties and general conduct	Dismissed	Misconduct Hearing
Aug 09	PC Male	Discreditable conduct	Final written warning	Misconduct meeting
Nov 09	PC Male	Performance of duties	Written warning	Misconduct meeting
Nov 09	Sergeant male	Performance of duties	Management advice	
Nov 09	Sergeant male	Duties and responsibilities	Management advice	Misconduct meeting
Jan 10	PC Male	Duties and Responsibilities	Written warning	Misconduct meeting
Feb 10	PC Male	Authority, Respect and Courtesy	Management advice	Misconduct meeting
Feb 10	PC Male	Duties and Responsibilities	Management advice	Misconduct meeting
Feb 10	PC Male	Duties and Responsibilities	Management advice	Misconduct meeting
Feb 10	PC Female	Duties and Responsibilities	Management advice	Misconduct meeting 3
Feb 10	PC Male	General conduct x2, politeness and tolerance	Dismissed	Misconduct Hearing
Mar 10	PC Male	Misuse of the force electronic & communication policy	Written warning	Misconduct meeting
Apr 10	Inspector male	Orders and Instructions	Management advice	Misconduct meeting

Constabulary Table 3.2 Cont.

Date	Employee Type	Nature	Outcome of internal procedures	Comment
Jun 10	PC Male	Discreditable conduct	Final Written warning	Misconduct Hearing
Jun 10	PC Male	Discreditable conduct	Final Written warning	Misconduct Hearing
Jun 10	PC Male	Misuse of the force electronic & communication policy	Management advice	Misconduct meeting
Jul 10	PC Male	Authority, Respect and Courtesy	Management advice	Misconduct meeting
Sep 10	PC Male	Duties and responsibilities	Management advice	Misconduct meeting
Dec 10	PC Male	Honesty and integrity	Dismissed	Misconduct Hearing
Jan 11	PC Male	Misuse of police vehicle	Management advice	Misconduct meeting
Feb 11	PC Male	Discreditable conduct	Dismissed	Misconduct Hearing
Feb 11	Inspector Male	Discreditable conduct	Final written warning	Misconduct meeting
Feb 11	Chief Inspector Male	Discreditable conduct	Final written warning	Misconduct meeting

Constabulary 2007–12

The table above, Constabulary Table 3.2, details the discipline areas from male and female police officers during the 2007–11 period. In 2007, we see that only male officers were disciplined. Three male officers were disciplined for lawful orders/general conduct (1), abuse of authority and general conduct (1), and performance of duties/lawful orders (1). In 2007, in the Constabulary police area, 3 male officers were disciplined, with no female officers disciplined. In 2008, it was 14 male officers in comparison to two female officers, and 2009 saw 18 males and 1 female officer disciplined. The year 2010 involved 13 male officers and 1 female, while 2011 included 4 male officers and no females, and in 2012 it was 17 males and 1 female.

70 *Feminist use of Freedom of Information*

Constabulary 2008

In 2008, one female officer was disciplined for duties and responsibilities (1), while fifteen male officers were disciplined during this same period. They were disciplined for failure in duty (4), misuse of force electronic and communication policy (1), neglect of duty (1), abuse of authority (1), politeness and tolerance (1), performance of duties (2), abuse of authority and general conduct (1), criminal conviction (2), duties and responsibilities (1), and misuse of the Police National Computer (PNC), performance of duties, and general conduct (1).

Constabulary 2009

In 2009, in this service area only one female officer was disciplined for duties and responsibilities (1), while eighteen men were disciplined for breaches including discreditable conduct (5), performance of duties (4), performance of duties and general conduct (1), duties and responsibilities (6), failure in duty (1), and misuse of the electronic communication policy (1).

Constabulary 2010

In the 2010 data, one female was disciplined for duties and responsibilities (1), while thirteen men were disciplined for duties and responsibilities (4), honesty and integrity (1), authority, respect, and courtesy (2), general conduct, politeness, and tolerance (1), misuse of force electronic and communication policy (2), orders and instructions (1), and discreditable conduct (2).

Constabulary 2011

In 2011, all four officers disciplined up to February were male, for misuse of police vehicle (1) and discreditable conduct (3).

In Constabulary Table 3.3 on page 71, between 2011 and 2012, only one female was disciplined for discreditable conduct (1), while male officers were disciplined for discreditable conduct (1), duties and responsibilities (10), failure in duty (1), followed by two errors in the records from the Police, where they are cited under breach as male constable (5) in bold, August and October 2011.

Feminist use of Freedom of Information 71

Constabulary Table 3.3 All serving officers disciplined, breach, and male and female 2011–12

Date of Hearing or Meeting 2011/12	Rank/Gender	Breach	Outcome
Feb-11	Male Inspector	Discreditable Conduct	Final Written Warning
April-11	2 Male Constables	Duties and Responsibilities	1. Written warning 2. Management Action
June-11	Male Constable	Duties and Responsibilities	Final Written Warning
Aug-11	**Male Chief Inspector/ Male Inspector/ Male Sergeant/Male Constable**	**Male Constable ERROR**	**Final Written Warning**
Aug-11	Male Constable	Failure in Duty	Management Advice
Oct-11	**Male Constable**	**Male Constable ERROR**	**Final Written Warning**
Sep-11	Male Inspector	Duties and Responsibilities	Management Advice
Mar-12	Male Sergeant	Duties and Responsibilities	Management Advice
Feb-12	Male Constable	Duties and Responsibilities	Management Action
Feb-12	Female Constable	Discreditable Conduct	Management Advice
Apr-12	Male Chief Inspector/ Male Inspector/ Male Sergeant/ Male Constable	Duties and Responsibilities	Management Advice

Force Police area

Force Table 3.1 Breach type, male and female officers 2007–12

Year >	2007/8		2008/9		2009/0		2010/1		2011/2		TOTALS	
Details	F	M	F	M	F	M	F	M	F	M	F	M
Drink Driving									1	1	1	1
Sharing inappropriate comments on Facebook									1	0	1	
Misuse of IRIS				2				1		4	0	7

(continued)

72 Feminist use of Freedom of Information

Force Table 3.1 Cont.

Year >	2007/8		2008/9		2009/0		2010/1		2011/2		TOTALS	
Details	F	M	F	M	F	M	F	M	F	M	F	M
Sexual offences/ harassment/misconduct									1		0	1
Harassment									1		0	1
Off duty altercation/ conduct								1	1		0	2
Confidentiality/ inappropriate association									1		0	1
Custody issues							1	1			1	1
Misconduct in public office/Data Protection Act								1			0	1
Serious neglect of duty (road policing incidents)								1			0	1
Prisoner escape								2			0	2
Assisting breach of bail conditions								1			0	1
Equality and diversity breach								1			0	1
Inappropriate relationship with crime victim				3				1			0	4
Excessive force								1			0	1
Moved wiper from police to own vehicle								1			0	1
Gained information by using police status		1						1			0	2
Failed to properly dispose of substance								1			0	1
Issues around business interest								1			0	1
Failure to secure crime resulting in theft/loss								1			0	1
Obtaining shell points on police card								1			0	1
No excise licence/ attachment of earnings order							1				1	0
Disclosed confidential information						1					0	1
Incivility						1					0	1
Bankruptcy						1					0	1
Unauthorised absence from duty						1					0	1

Feminist use of Freedom of Information 73

Force Table 3.1 Cont.

Year >	2007/8		2008/9		2009/0		2010/1		2011/2		TOTALS	
Details	F	M	F	M	F	M	F	M	F	M	F	M
Failure to investigate properly					1						1	0
Using mobile when driving and dishonesty					1						1	0
Police vehicle accident				1	1						1	1
Sending inappropriate images via force email					1						1	0
Custody issues relating to death in custody			1	1							1	1
Drugs				1							0	1
False statement on application form				1							0	1
Domestic violence				1							0	1
Identity parade irregularities	1										1	0
Taking a post-mortem photo and distributing it				1							0	1
Totals	**1**	**5**	**1**	**7**	**4**	**4**	**2**	**17**	**1**	**10**	**9**	**43**

Force 2007

The female officer disciplined in 2007–08 for irregularities in relation to an identification parade brings to mind the 23 policewomen data (Cunningham and Ramshaw 2020) and Chapter 2 where uniform was seen as a site of challenge and resistance for these policewomen, and I would have liked further details regarding this breach in order to make an informed conclusion, so this lack of detail in relation to offences can be seen as another limitation of the study.

Force 2008

It is evident from the table (Force Table 3.1) above that in four of the five years, men were disproportionately involved/apprehended for disciplinary offences. Moreover, the nature of men's offences more frequently concerned an abuse of power – forming inappropriate relationships with victims of crime being one example, domestic violence another. A notable exception to this, however, involved one of the most serious breaches seen within this data – the proceedings that followed a death in custody in 2008/09 – which involved a policeman and a policewoman.

74 *Feminist use of Freedom of Information*

Force 2009

Only in 2009/10 were the numbers of policemen and policewomen equal, meaning an over-representation of women given the different proportions of females and males within the Force police area. The data from 2009/10 is interesting because it appears to illustrate that female officers can be involved in similar breaches to male officers, such as the sharing of an image and a police vehicle accident.

Importantly, the data also illustrates dishonesty, in contrast to the stereotype of honesty noted earlier in relation to policewomen and which contrasts with earlier ideas of women and their feminine moral superiority (Jackson, 2006).

The male officers' involvement in breaches is more disturbing alongside the dishonesty of making a false application; however, the main differences are the misuse of the Police computer for personal reasons, which women officers have not been found to have been involved in, and domestic violence, which was also cited in the investigation into Victoria Police in Australia (2019), and drugs.

Between 2011 and 2012, a female was involved in drunk driving as was a male officer during this same period. However, all of the other offences during this period involved male officers and included inappropriate comments on Facebook (1), and misuse of the police data system called IRIS (4). Important differences in types of offence include the aggressive interpersonal nature of the other male officers' involvement in offences, which include allegation of potential sexual offences, harassment and conduct issues on and off duty (1), harassment (1), off-duty

Force Table 3.2 Breach type, male and female 2011–12

01/04/2011–31/03/2012	
Details	*Gender*
Drink Driving	Female
Drink Driving	Male
Inappropriate comments on Facebook	Male
Misuse of IRIS	Male
Allegation of potential sexual offences, harassment and conduct issues on and off duty	Male
Misuse of IRIS	Male
Misuse of IRIS	Male
Harassment	Male
Off Duty Altercation	Male
Misuse of IRIS	Male
Confidentiality issues and inappropriate association	Male

Feminist use of Freedom of Information 75

Force Table 3.3 Cases upheld, breach, male and female

Details	Gender	Upheld
Drink Driving	Female	Yes
Drink Driving	Male	Yes
Inappropriate comments on Facebook	Male	Yes
Misuse of IRIS	Male	Yes
Allegation of potential sexual offences, harassment and conduct issues on and off duty	Male	Yes
Misuse of IRIS	Male	Yes
Misuse of IRIS	Male	Yes
Harassment	Male	Yes
Off Duty Altercation	Male	Yes
Misuse of IRIS	Male	Yes
Confidentiality issues and inappropriate association	Male	Yes

altercation (1), and confidentiality issues and inappropriate association (1). During this period in this police service area, women did not get involved with such offences, though drink driving has the potential for causing massive harm and/or death to others. These cases were all upheld, as seen in the table above (Force Table 3.3).

Within this period of 2010–11, only two female officers were disciplined, and the offences were custody issues (1) and no excise license and attachment of earnings order (1). In contrast, their male colleagues were involved with matters ranging from custody issues (1), failure to properly dispose of substance (1), misuse of IRIS (1), obtaining of Shell points on a police card (1), removal of windscreen wiper from police vehicle for use on own vehicle (1), failure to secure crime properly resulting in its theft/loss (1), issues surrounding business interest, and equality and diversity (1) to, at the other end of the scale, criminal investigation involving misconduct in a Public Office and matters relating to Sec. 55 of the Data Protection Act (1), allegation of serious neglect of duty in relation to his enquiries into serious road policing incidents (1), prisoner escape (2), assisting father-in-law to breach his bail conditions by attending home address (1), inappropriate relationship with victim of crime (1), off-duty conduct outside a pub (1), excessive use of force (1), and facilitation of obtaining information required by way of abusing his status as a police officer (1).

Between 2009 and 2010 in this service area, as many female (4) as male (4) officers were disciplined. The male officers were involved in disclosing confidential information (1), incivility (1), declaring bankruptcy (1), and unauthorised absence from duty (1), whereas their female peers

76 *Feminist use of Freedom of Information*

Force Table 3.4 Cases upheld, breach, male and female 2010–11

Details	Upheld	Gender
Custody Issues	Yes	Male
		Female
Criminal investigation involving misconduct in a Public Office and matters relating Sec 55 of the Data Protection Act (See Reg 15)	Yes	Male
Allegation of serious neglect of duty in relation to his enquiries into serious road policing incidents	Yes	Male
Prisoner escape	Yes	Male
		Male
Officer has assisted his father in law to breach his bail conditions by attending her home address	Yes	Male
Equality and Diversity	Yes	Male
Inappropriate relationship with victim of crime	Yes	Male
Off-duty conduct outside a pub	Yes	Male
Excessive force	Yes	Male
Failed to properly dispose of substance	Yes	Male
Issues surround business interest	Yes	Male
Facilitated obtaining information you required by way of abusing your status as a Police Officer	Yes	Male
Removed windscreen wiper from police vehicle for use on own vehicle	Yes	Male
Failed to secure crime properly resulting in its theft/ loss	Yes	Male
Obtaining Shell points on a police card	Yes	Male
No excise licence and attachment of earnings order	Yes	Female
Misuse of IRIS	Yes	Male

Note: 01/ 04/ 2011–31/ 03/ 2012. Typo Error found from the Force Police Data, should be 2010 and 2011.

Force Table 3.5 Cases upheld, breach, male and female 2009–10

Details	Upheld	Gender
Disclosed confidential information	Yes	Male
Incivility	Yes	Male
Declared Bankrupt	Yes	Male
Unauthorised absence from duty	Yes	Male
Failed to investigate properly	Yes	Female
Used mobile phone when driving, then lied about it	Yes	Female
Police vehicle accident	Yes	Female
Sent inappropriate images via the force email system	Yes	Female

Feminist use of Freedom of Information 77

Force Table 3.6 Cases upheld, breach, male and female 2008–09

Details	Upheld	Gender
Inappropriate relationships with victims of crime	Yes	Male
		Male
		Male
Custody issues relating to a death in custody	Yes	Male
		Female
Misuse of IRIS	Yes	Male
Police vehicle accident	Yes	Male
Misuse of IRIS	Yes	Male

were disciplined for failure to investigate properly (1), use of a mobile phone then lying about it (1), police vehicle accident (1), and sending inappropriate images via the Force email system (1). This data appears to illustrate that female officers can be involved in some similar breaches to male officers, such as the sharing of an image (see Constabulary above) and police vehicle accident (see Constabulary above), and importantly again illustrates dishonesty in contrast to the stereotype of honesty noted earlier in relation to policewomen.

During 2008 to 2009, only one female was disciplined and this for the most serious offence, alongside a male colleague, for custody issues relating to a death in custody (2). Male officers were disciplined for misuse of IRIS (2), police vehicle accident (1), and inappropriate relationships with victims of crime (3). This data illustrates the most serious breach that a female officer was involved in together with her male colleague, which requires acknowledgement even if we do not have further details, and the male officers were involved in breaches of misuse of IRIS and police vehicle accident, and also three policemen were disciplined in relation to having inappropriate relationships with victims of crime, again an abuse of power.

The tables illustrate that in 2007–08, see page 78, one female was disciplined in comparison to five male officers, while 2008–09 see above shows again one female officer disciplined in contrast to seven male officers during the same period. In 2009–10, four female officers and four male officers were disciplined, and in 2010–11, see pages 75 and 76, two females were disciplined, while seventeen male officers were. Finally, 2011–12 saw one female officer disciplined, while ten male officers were disciplined, see page 74.

In 2007 to 2008, only one female officer was disciplined for irregularities in relation to an identification parade (1), while in contrast her five male colleagues were disciplined for taking a photograph at

78   *Feminist use of Freedom of Information*

Force Table 3.7 Cases upheld, breach, male and female 2007–08

Details	Upheld	Gender
Took a photograph at a post-mortem and distributed it	Yes	Male
Made false statement on application form	Yes	Male
Carried out PNC check for personal reasons	Yes	Male
Domestic Violence	Yes	Male
Irregularities in relation to an identification parade	Yes	Female
Drugs	Yes	Male

a post-mortem and distributing it (1), making a false statement on an application form (1), carrying out a PNC check for personal reasons (1), domestic violence (1), and drugs (1).

The female officer who was disciplined in this year for irregularities in relation to an identification parade brings to mind the snapshot of the 23 policewomen data (Cunningham and Ramshaw 2020) and Chapter 2, where uniform was seen as a site of challenge and resistance for these policewomen, and I would have liked further detail regarding this breach in order to make an informed conclusion. The male officers' involvement in breaches is more disturbing on the whole, but the sharing of the post-mortem image can be seen as similar to the policewoman example, alongside the dishonesty of making a false application; however, the main differences are the misuse of the police computer for personal reasons, which women officers have not been seen to have been involved in; domestic violence, which was also cited in the investigation into Victoria Police in Australia (VEOHRC, Phase 3, 2019); and drugs.

For the Constabulary police area, the over-representation of men in the data is very marked, just as Rabe-Hemp had suggested (Rabe-Hemp, 2008b). Just three policewomen faced disciplinary action in the period – less than 6 per cent of the total. Moreover, this was despite Constabulary having a higher proportion of women officers than the national average.

Findings and discussion

Like Westmarland and Rowe's study (2018) which explored questions of police ethics and integrity, I also utilised data records from three police service areas to explore policewomen's and policemen's disciplinary records. Westmarland and Rowe (2018) found no difference between policewomen and policemen reporting misdeeds; however, my study into policemen's and policewomen's disciplinary records did illustrate

Feminist use of Freedom of Information 79

some key differences in the kinds of disciplinary offences they were involved in.

The information I asked the three service areas for was the number of upheld disciplinary offences and the nature of the breach per year from 2006 to 2011, broken down into female and male officer numbers. I also asked for this information for the year 2011–12. They noted that a written warning could be given under the old regulations and so these have been included as disciplinary. They also explained that the old regulations and the new regulations have different breaches for pre-Taylor and new Taylor cases.

The kinds of offences that officers were disciplined for during this time frame and across all three force areas ranged from using a police vehicle window wiper on one's own vehicle and taking points for filling petrol in police vehicles, to lack of duty resulting in a death in custody. Comparing and contrasting findings was difficult given the different headings that offences came under, the changes in offence types, and the level of detail, or lack of it that is provided from different police forces.

Digging down into the data, what I did find was that firstly, the smaller numbers of women disciplined in the three force areas across these years may fit with the conclusions of Rabe-Hemp (2008b), in that some of the figures seen are astonishingly low for women officers, and that this has important conclusions in relation to police accountability. This has been suggested to be the case because women officers were seen as outsiders, as Rabe-Hemp, (2008b) argued as well as findings from Barnes, Beaulieu, and Saxton showed, who in their study confirmed women officers were less likely to be involved with corruption and criminal networks and also that their behaviour is more risk averse (Barnes, Beaulieu, and Saxton, 2017: 9). It could be that it is the case women are involved in fewer offences because women, even as police officers, would not in patriarchal society be considered as powerful, and as they do not have male privilege, they cannot abuse it. These findings certainly confirm that women police officers appear to have a different style of policing to their male peers. One suggestion I would add is that police disciplinary offence types should include misogyny as this would allow clear identification of some of the offences which would fall into this bracket. Any of the offences which did fall into this bracket should also set off alarm bells within policing, since men who have imbibed such outdated notions in relation to the nature of women and girls should be seen as potential threats to them. At the very least, police training and education really need to explore such notions and challenge these ideas early on, sending a clear message to all officers. Stinson, Todak, and Dodge (2013), who explored officer misdeeds via a Google News and

80   *Feminist use of Freedom of Information*

Google Alerts media data collection approach found, as I did, a difference in the misdeeds/offences between policewomen and policemen with women involved in profit-related crime as opposed to policemen, who were involved in sexual or violent and sexual violence crime.

Unfortunately, the data from Service does not go into the same details as Constabulary and Force data, which makes it difficult to contrast the two groups of police. This means that it limits what I can say and how this fits with the two other areas, especially in relation to the misuse of the force computer system and the involvement in relationships with victims of crime, which I could clearly see in the other force areas. What I can illustrate is that in Service Table 3.7, I found that male officers are disciplined much more often than females, and that, just as Roman (2020) argued in relation to policing in the United States, male officers were more involved in abuse of authority and misuse of force than their female peers were (See Service Table 3.2, where the highlighted contrast with policewomen is 0).

In the Constabulary area, some similarities in terms of policewomen's and policemen's involvement in offence types, such as the sharing of an image and also police vehicle offences, are also seen in the Force area, with a post-mortem picture that was shared. I also found the misuse of the police computer for personal use could be seen in both the Constabulary and Force areas in relation to policemen, but not policewomen. This misuse of police computer systems by policemen for personal use was also seen in Australia (Bucci, 2020).

In Force, there was a death in custody case during this period which involved both a policewoman and policeman who were disciplined. Force also saw cases of sexual offences, harassment, off-duty altercations, inappropriate comments on Facebook, drugs, and inappropriate relationships with victims of crime, like the disciplinary offences seen recently in Australia (Bucci, 2020) and the sharing of an inappropriate image (by a policewoman), as noted above. The final comparison of Force with Victoria in Australia was the Domestic Violence and Abuse case (VEOHRC, Phase 3, 2019).

The data I found certainly contrasts with the ideas from Reece and Strange (2019), whose work Laverick had cited (2021), in relation to the initial fears that when women joined the police, they would form inappropriate relationships with policemen and suspects. This research illustrates, in contrast to this fear, that it is inappropriate relationships between policemen and vulnerable victims of crime, not policewomen, that can clearly be noted in the data. While these relations have been noted by the IPOC (2020), further longitudinal studies on police behaviours, ethics, and disciplines are required in a much larger study.

Feminist use of Freedom of Information 81

I would suggest that a national review of police disciplinary behaviour in England and Wales be undertaken to see what the findings are across England and Wales. This is especially relevant given the examples of exposing the penis, relationships with junior staff, inappropriate comments, sexual harassment, database searches for personal use, and sexual relationships with victims of crime, as seen in the disciplinary data in the Australian case (Bucci, 2020). Differences could be seen in policemen's and policewomen's discipline records in relation to the use of force too. While Simpson and Croft's (2020) findings suggest that women officers in uniform are perceived as being as aggressive as men, the findings about women officers and their actual disciplinary records illustrate a difference between perception of aggression and practice.

These findings show that toxic masculinity and misogyny can still be seen to inform the kinds of offences that male police officers are involved in. The Australian investigation and the recent real-world example of the news report about the reinstated officer in Victoria (Bucci, 2020) illustrate that there is a long way to go in terms of successfully dealing with these officers. Backlash against change alongside the continuance of the worst elements of 'police culture' can also be seen in policing in England and Wales in these findings. My findings were confirmed by those of Stinson, Todak, and Dodge (2013), who earlier found in their study in America that while policewomen's offences fell into the 'profit-related' category on the whole, this was in contrast to policemen's offences, which were seen to be more often in the 'sex-related' or 'violence-related' and sexual violence categories. This worrying trend seen in America, Australia, and England and Wales, as illustrated in findings in each of these areas, illustrates a problem with misogyny within police culture. Utilising an intersectional feminist lens allows this discussion about how these findings fit in patriarchal society alongside expectations about the nature of woman and man. Long after Wollstonecraft's critique of inequality in the eighteenth century in England, these findings illustrate that misogyny still informs society in general, and in particular is mirrored in these offence types in worldwide policing disciplinary examples today, illustrating the globalisation of police culture as explained by Brown and Heidensohn (2000).

In the last few days of writing this book, a young woman, Sarah Everard, who had been missing after walking home from her friend's house in London, was found murdered. The main suspect in this case is a serving Metropolitan Police Officer, Wayne Couzens, who has been arrested and charged, along with a female who allegedly assisted an offender. It has been confirmed in the news that this officer had been involved in a sexual offence of indecent exposure days before the alleged

82 *Feminist use of Freedom of Information*

kidnap and murder of Sarah Everard (Chakrabarti, 2021). This whole shocking case has ignited debate about how women have had to get used to, and live with the constant threat of male violence in everyday life. While unions and women's groups (Northern TUC, March 13, 2021) were attempting to reclaim the streets, the police were worried that a vigil for Sarah would break lockdown measures, and so approached the courts for a decision, which resulted in a suggestion that both sides work together. This case impacts on the feeling of safety of all women when regardless of the care taken by them to avoid harm, this woman was murdered by a police officer whose job is to keep all citizens safe. The Metropolitan Police Service (MPS) are undoubtedly as shocked as everyone else about this.

Details of officer discipline on a national level require outside full and rigorous scrutiny if any attempt at legitimacy in policing is to be approached, and where predatory behaviours from officers are found, they should be clearly dealt with so that these behaviours do not become emboldened. This full and rigorous discipline was not evidenced recently in England and Wales when the IOPC were considered ineffective, as fewer than one in ten police officers were fired after gross misconduct in England and Wales (Busby, 2021). I would suggest, given the findings here, and issues in relation to police discipline, that if officers are flagged up as engaging in misogynistic offences and behaviours, this should be an indicator that there is potential for worse misdeeds or offences. An editorial in *The Guardian* (March 11, 2021) suggested that without safety for women and girls, there can be no equality, and they cite levels of harassment and violence against women and girls from a UK UN study. They note that six women and a little girl were reported killed in the period Sarah Everard went missing. Importantly, they suggest legislative change, but also change in terms of our expectations for girls and boys, where girls should not have to shrink their lives to remain safe, and where boys should respect girls and women and should challenge when this is not happening. In Australia, Gorman (2021) expected demonstrations and protests against gendered discrimination and violence against women in March 2021 in the March4justice. Even within the Sarah Everard murder investigation a probationer police officer was removed from public-facing duties after sharing an inappropriate graphic via WhatsApp with his colleagues (Dodd, 2021). He had been involved in the search for Sarah Everard, and was reported by his colleagues for this communication. Disturbingly, this was a relatively new police officer displaying this misogynistic behaviour, which confirms that this is not just a case of being informed by police culture,

Feminist use of Freedom of Information 83

as he is new; rather, this illustrates that such notions prevail in society and are taken on board by some men who behave in a way which illustrates that they are happy to dehumanise women in their everyday life and work. *The Observer* used Freedom of Information requests to obtain disciplinary data in relation to MPS officers. Their FOI study confirmed similar findings to mine in that there were cases involving an officer having sexual intercourse with a rape victim, domestic violence and abuse, and misogynistic offences against women in society by policemen (Townsend and Jayanetti, 2021). This again illustrates 'institutional misogyny' as a major problem alongside what we have seen in relation to institutional racism, and as illustrated in *The Observer* report as well as seen in my FOI data, the misogynistic police culture intensified at the intersections of race and gender. Worryingly, if Dick does not acknowledge institutional racism in MPS, it is unlikely she will accept institutional misogyny either.

Only with a feminist perspective that is aware of the struggle and continual backlash that feminism has faced and continues to face, and the current issues in relation to public order policing today, especially as recently witnessed with the manhandling and rough police tactics used at the peaceful vigil for Sarah Everard at Clapham Common in London (March 2021), can policing retain legitimacy and public confidence for all citizens. With the shift to a more authoritarian approach to policing protests requested by Priti Patel and Her Majesty's Inspectorate of Constabulary and Fire and Rescue Services (HMICFRS) (Siddiqui, 2021) and during the COVID-19 pandemic, attempts to curb the human rights of citizens to protest are being made within the police, crime, sentencing, and courts bill 2021. This bill extends stop and search powers and limits demonstrations like Black Lives Matter (BLM) and Extinction Rebellion (XR). The disturbing reality from the fourth female home secretary and the first female MPS commissioner is that they are leading this call for stronger police powers. Chakrobarti (2021) reminds in her opinion piece, that these women pushing for stronger state action in relation to citizens is a bitter feminist irony, and that it is the system that requires change, not simply the faces within it. In the same week as Meghan Markle came under racist attack and we celebrated International Women's Day in March 2021, the shameful events of Saturday, March 13, at Clapham Common where females protesting against male violence and misogyny were manhandled by the police illustrates a long way for policing to go in England and Wales. Calls for the resignation of Dick have been made (Chakrobarti, 2021) as well as women's groups suggesting they no longer have confidence in her leadership of MPS.

84 *Feminist use of Freedom of Information*

The brutal murder of Sarah Everard allegedly by a serving police officer, has sparked a moment in England and Wales where women have noted their own everyday negotiation of their space in relation to their own safety and their continual avoidance of their own victimisation, which is unacceptable, unequal, and requires a feminist understanding and response. Exposure to everyday sexism and racism may be on the agenda for a while, and perhaps those who will produce policy in relation to opposing Violence Against Women and Girls (VAWG) should look at these debates again and take these into account when addressing these perspectives. Review of policing practice in England and Wales is urgently required to address the misogyny within policing (which has been seen in some of the examples within this book to persist in America and Australia as well as England and Wales), to prevent these outdated ideas about the nature of woman still informing male harassment, violence against, and the murder of, women. The police got this operation wrong, and even given the 'fiendishly hard' balance of public order and the pandemic as described by Dick (BBC News, March 15, 2021), the women at the peaceful vigil to remember Sarah and to protest about male violence against them in society should not have been met with police manhandling and handcuffs.

Summary

This chapter has explored ideas about whether policewomen are different, and as such whether they bring something different to the role of policing. It was seen within the different types of misdeeds that they were involved in, in contrast to their male peers, that policewomen behaved differently to policemen. Their style of policing can also be seen as being different to that from their male peers which causes fewer problems and more faith on the part of citizens. Policemen were seen to have abused their position informed by ideas of masculinity, misogyny, and patriarchal power to engage in relationships with victims of crime who were vulnerable, or in domestic violence or sexual violence.

Adding women to build legitimacy in policing, as argued by Barnes, Beaulieu and Saxton (2017), may help policing legitimacy, but will not be a panacea to addressing citizen concerns with policing. I would argue adding feminists to review policing practice including discipline, alongside more representative police officers, will help citizens have faith in policing. Only these measures with an intersectional feminist challenge and critique, and review of these records will help policing move beyond the everyday racism and misogyny seen within policing today and towards the legitimacy of the police. The extraordinary catalogue of sexual misconduct within the MPS uncovered by the use of FOI requests by *The Observer* confirms the levels of misogyny and reinforces my conclusions that a feminist intersectional critique of police disciplinary records is a vital step to challenge and change this culture.

4 Conclusions and summary

In Chapter 1, I explored the notions of sameness and difference as used by both Wollstonecraft and her contemporary thinkers and suggested that these ideas remain alive and well now, and can be seen in contemporary narratives about women in the police. I argued Wollstonecraft is constricted in the eighteenth century to avoiding both crippling 'difference' arguments in relation to the nature of women in order to gain any idea of equality in the future. I illustrate how these difference arguments of her peers win out for centuries and examine discussions of how to resolve this dilemma, which has taken ideas from Scott (1988), Squires (2000, 2003, 2007), and Pateman (1988: 1995) who have devoted due care, time, attention, and space to these important concepts and their use. I disagree with Scott's suggestion (1988) that we should stop tracing these arguments, suggesting we should still keep watch where these arguments emerge in narratives as they still can add to our understanding and analysis of the place of policewomen. I also suggest that in terms of identity, policewomen themselves may internalise these ideas and may in turn inform their own style of policing and the type of police officer they can be seen as, and importantly see themselves as either Police WOMAN or POLICE woman for instance as in Martin's study (1980). However, the misogyny that underlies the notions of what a woman is, continues far beyond Wollstonecraft's era in wider society and this is amplified and reflected within the culture of policing now.

In Chapter 2, I followed the arguments of difference and sameness as they have reappeared within the policing literature. I reassessed a data set of policing to see how these arguments play out given the findings about the nature of woman in this study. I now find that notions of difference of officers have informed and entrenched the male ideal and norm of police officer, and that this has had, and continues to have, consequences such as the major differences in uniform. Male officers' ideas of the different nature of woman were illustrated

DOI: 10.4324/9781003149156-5

Conclusions and summary 87

in the policewoman's uniform. I note women officers' historical resistance to wearing uncomfortable and inappropriate uniform as well as acknowledging that this image of the male ideal norm of police officer remains, and can be seen in the way that new police 'kit' has been designed, reflecting this male design rather than being designed for the different body shapes of male and female officers. Uniform has more recently attempted to be more about utility and sameness of combat trousers and T-shirts for all officers, but still requires critique such as in relation to using the new body-cam kit. I suggest further research is required especially in terms of the trust and representation of policing in England and Wales.

I move on to explore these ideas using an example of Australia where I examine narratives about the sameness and difference of officers which have continued alongside ideas about where they should be deployed. Secondly, I noted the work of an investigation several decades after Wilkinson and Froyland's (1996) discussion about the sameness and difference of women police officers. This third review of policing in Victoria (VEOHRC, Phase 3, 2019) illustrated that many of the issues about recruitment and retention of policewomen remain relevant across this time period as seen in both England and Wales and Australia. One of the major contrasts to Wilkinson and Froyland's (1996) paper was the feminist stance of acknowledging that policewomen were discriminated against, and that issues such as disciplinary approaches to sexism and changes in structural support to allow for equality through difference, such as flexible working for parents, were clearly illustrated in the Victorian report. Ideas about structural support, such as flexible working for parents, which can offer policewomen the same opportunities to actualise the equality to remain at work when they have families, can be seen decades later when we get the investigation in Australia (VEOHRC, Phase 3, 2019). The report notes the vigorous recent attempts they make within their investigation into policing culture and harm to make positive changes in order to benefit policing for all the officers as well as for Australian citizens, and suggests it will, like feminism, face a backlash. This transformative change, I argue, essentially consists of a feminist approach of acknowledging gender inequality exists and is located deeply in misogynistic notions about the nature and abilities of woman. Challenging these outdated notions and the sexism and harassment which accompany these ideas across policing culture, based on the ideal male, active, and deeply misogynistic model of policing, is vital in this review of policing along with the equal opportunities and human rights approach I argue constitutes a feminist review. I suggest Crenshaw's (2017) ideas about the use of an intersectional lens could be utilised in

88   *Conclusions and summary*

a rigorous review of policing. As well as seeking attitudinal change, as feminists do, this also requires a reworking of practices such as flexibility of work, childcare, pay, and pension areas so that structures will not discriminate against policewomen either.

In Chapter 3, I used an innovative research method of asking for and being given FOI information about the officers in three service areas who have been disciplined over a five-year period. Here I find that there are more male officers, notwithstanding the research caveats involved, engaging more often in disciplinary offences, and that there are some different types of offences committed by them in contrast to women officers. The kinds of offences which illustrate an abuse of power relationship by policemen in cases such as with domestic violence or having inappropriate relations with victims of crime do not appear in the data in relation to women officers. Sadly, there are any number of examples which illustrate the entrenched misogyny within our society, and these are mirrored and reflected in the disciplinary data from the police officers in my study. While we saw some similarities of offence type, such as the sharing of inappropriate images, and duty and responsibility offences as well as police vehicle offences and even a death in custody offence, we did not witness female abuse of power and authority in forming inappropriate relationships or female abuse of force in ways which were seen in the policemen sample. This difference is not due to the nature of woman; however, I argue it is a different style of policing which is embodied by policewomen, who are not used to a position of power within patriarchal society. Policewomen's position reflects the patriarchy embedded within our society, is amplified within police culture, and informs their risk averseness and outsider status as non-macho, non-misogynistic, and non-aggressive. These elements of policewomen inform the style of policing policewomen contribute, as seen with neighbourhood policing approaches which built on links between police officers in their communities. While neighbourhood and community policing has shifted once more, this style of policing points to the effectiveness of women in policing in terms of building police relations based on trust and legitimacy, as needed across policing worldwide (Waugh, Ede, and Alley, 1998).

Waugh, Ede, and Alley's (1998) study in Queensland Australia sought to explore whether policewomen were less likely to engage in misconduct or approve of it than policemen. For this study they used three sources, attitudinal surveys, police-initiated complaints, and public complaints against the police. Interestingly, they found that the attitudinal data showed similar results between officers, and that women were as likely to modify their views after spending time in the field. The police

Conclusions and summary   89

data illustrated a difference with male officers more likely to attract complaints. Overall they also found that policewomen were not inherently more ethical, but that their policing styles and behaviours were different. The suggestion that women were treated as different/other was also asserted in relation to why their behaviour was different. They cite confounding factors such as policewomen being less likely to be on the front line in explaining the disparity of male complaints (Waugh, Ede, and Alley, 1998). Rather than using essentialist arguments to explain these differences, research from Barnes, Beaulieu, and Saxton (2017) importantly highlights that women were more risk averse and were seen as and felt themselves to be outsiders, which could be part of the answer, and Barnes *et al.* note the difference in styles of policing used by women. The argument of male privilege in patriarchal society means that men generally, and male police officers in particular, are in a position of power and authority that women are unable to ever be in, even as policewomen. This power differential and abuse of power allows those policemen who are predatory to behave differently to policewomen and to abuse their position of power within the police misogyny which is institutionalised.

Conclusion

This book has traced ideas about the nature of women from the eighteenth century within the history of political thought in order to illustrate how these ideas and concepts still inform ideas of what women are and which informs ideas of what women can do. The earliest feminist thought remains resonant with exploring the place of women in policing and should inform transformative changes in policing practice. I sought to explore these ideas specifically in relation to women working within the police as this remains a male-dominated environment within which to work, even if the numbers are changing in England and Wales. I re-examine data of 23 policewomen in light of these ideas, and I also provide a discussion of similarity and change around issues of sameness and difference from two Australian studies with a couple of decades of time distance between them. The recent investigation in Victoria, which purports to use a Human Rights and Equality of Opportunity approach (VEOHRC, Phase 3, 2019), I suggest is actually a rigorous feminist review of policing which is extremely useful in beginning this long road to equality and fairness in society and policing. Unfortunately, I still see a gap between the aims of transformative change from the authors of the report and the actual practice of this, with the contrasting implications from the real-world example of the reinstatement of the officer whose

90 *Conclusions and summary*

behaviour was clearly grossly misogynistic (Bucci, 2020). The impact of this on citizen views of the legitimacy of policing are of central importance. I move on to adopt a new approach to exploring the kinds of disciplinary engagement that female and male officers are engaged in, across three police service areas in England and Wales over a five-year period. I find that there are some similar types of offences that both policewomen and policemen are involved in; however, where there is a marked difference, these include not just an offence against policing standards but also involve misogynistic abuse of power, in terms of status or force for their own benefit, which was not seen in the policewomen data. The problems associated with patriarchy and the embedded misogyny in our society have been unveiled again in cases which sadly show that women are not safe, celebrating a birthday in a park, or walking home from a friend's house. That women's and girls' lives are still at risk within the home as well as within society from men, and that their deaths are still read out each year in the House of Commons by Labour's Shadow Domestic Violence Minister, Jess Phillips, who read out 118 names this International Women's Day, is unacceptable (Parliament TV, 2021). This illustration of misogynistic crimes from society requires justice, and can clearly also be seen and amplified in policing culture, which includes the types of male behaviours and the breaches of standards of behaviour they are involved in, in contrast to female officers. It is only those male officers who feel they have this power, who can go on to abuse it. Women officers may be seen as having more power than women in society but will never, as women, be seen as powerful, especially in the way that male officers will do. The FOI from *The Observer* confirms my own FOI findings of the grim examples of policemen who have been disciplined for rape, sexual abuse, and domestic violence and abuse (Townsend and Jayanetti, 2021). As hooks (2000) argued, it is men who benefit the most from patriarchy. It appears we need a feminist review and critique of policing to keep a focus on attempts to change this culture and the problems associated with it. The pointers from Waugh, Ede, and Alley (1998) would be a start,

> Arguably, police services could benefit from examining more closely, the ways in which skilled policewomen, perform their duties and then educating male police officers in these techniques.
>
> (Waugh, Ede, and Alley, 1998: 298)

England and Wales need to look to Australia for how to develop the road map forward for policing and take an equal opportunities and human

Conclusions and summary 91

rights, feminist approach (VEOHRC, Phase 3, 2019). Furthermore, it is time to no longer shy away from using this 'f' word which, together with an intersectionality lens, could provide the best chance of moving from soundbite to road map, which can bring transformative change in supporting those diverse police members to remain within policing, and move towards real representation. However, strengthening legislation, as well as being fearless in the practice of transformational change and sending the right signals to all police staff, has been seen as equally as important as the will for this change to take place. A feminist-informed intersectional approach to reviewing policing would be the favoured approach to trying to alter the stranglehold of toxic masculinity that can be seen in policing culture still today. Only by dealing with the underlying issue of misogyny and stopping this from developing further within policing culture will we see change in police culture and the misogynistic culture within wider society. Women's approaches and styles of policing can also benefit all police officers and will help benefit discussions about police legitimacy and communication, as seen as vitally required in times of protests about the misuse of police force against black citizens, such as the Mark Duggan case, and in terms of the wider public order policing practice in relation to the death of Ian Tomalinson at the G20, for example. The use of community-style policing approaches have been seen to also use this feminised approach to policing (Skolnick, 2008), which may help rebuild police-citizen relationships over a period of time where they have been broken down. Where such policing initiatives have shifted from neighbourhood policing, this conclusion suggests a shift back to this as a major priority in relation to building a service for all its citizens to feel safe within. The disciplinary examples from the Victoria Police illustrate, like my findings, that male officer misdeeds are in some ways different from those that women officers are involved in, and I call for a disciplinary section entitled misogyny in police offences data, which could be vital in exploring the disciplinary offences and raising an alarm about these police offenders in relation to the safety of women and girls. Townsend and Jayanetti (2021) note that the FOI data did not indicate how many of the police offences went into the criminal justice system, which ought to be information which can be easily accessed. Much further use of feminist-informed education and training for serving and probationary officers is vital in illustrating such poor practice and power dynamics for all officers. Design of courses for police officers which illustrate where outdated notions about the supposed nature of woman and man come from, and which include feminist theory as well as real-world examples should highlight to police

92 *Conclusions and summary*

officers why these ideas are potentially so damaging to trust and legitimacy in policing.

Wollstonecraft's arguments for equality and sameness were of vital importance within her epoch to change ideas about the nature of woman and to allow ideas of education and citizenship for women. I suggest that now we need to supplement equality and legislation with a support framework that recognises and is inclusive of women's difference in terms of childbearing and caregiving so that we have an equal playing field. An intersectional analysis will explore difference and the way power plays across and between these for different people in terms of class, gender, race, and sexuality, for instance. Seeing and critiquing this difference as well as acknowledging them is the first step to challenge and change. Women's different approaches to policing have been seen to be more conducive to building public trust. Policemen, however, have been seen as still in a privileged position in a continuing patriarchal society, and the pervasive misogyny within current society can be seen to be amplified in policing with some of the real-world examples in the news and disciplinary data. An approach to challenging patriarchy which keeps our human rights central is as important now as it was for Wollstonecraft hundreds of years ago.

Moving to a more authoritarian approach to policing practice along the lines of crushing the right to noisy protest and arguing for change will put society and policing further back in terms of these human rights, which impacts on the freedom of citizens and the legitimacy of the police in the twenty-first century in England and Wales. Having women in positions of power within the government and MPS is not sufficient when they are continuing along Conservative and authoritarian lines, as Patel and Dick are, as this will oppose transformational change. Adding women to policing as suggested by Barnes, Beaulieu, and Saxton (2017) is not a panacea for addressing corruption and building legitimacy in policing. I argue it is feminists who are required precisely because they understand how misogyny is manifested and maintained. Only feminists will effectively challenge everyday sexism and everyday racism within society, as well as in policing, in order to bring about transformational change across police training, practice, and discipline areas. Only when underlying conditions are challenged and changed can we expect change in institutions like policing within society which requires continued feminist focus. In the wake of the murder of Sarah Everard, it appears that the domestic abuse bill may be amended to include a stalkers register and importantly include misogyny as a hate crime, even temporarily (Elgot, 2021). I hope this moment can be maintained and that misogyny will be included in police disciplinary records too, as an indicator of the threat of those carrying out those actions against women in policing, and women and girls in society. Wollstonecraft's call that it is justice rather than charity that is needed in the world, remains as resonant a cry today as it ever was, both for Sarah Everard and for women and girls everywhere.

Bibliography

Akkerman, T., and Stuurman, S. Eds. (1998) 'Introduction: feminism in European history'. In (Ed) Akkerman, T., and Stuurman, S. Perspectives on Feminist Political Thought. In *European History from the Middle Ages to the Present,* London, Routledge, 1–34.

Andrews, M., and Lomas, J. (2017) 'Home fronts, gender war and conflict'. *Women's History Review* 26(4): 523–7.

Ayling, J., Grabosky, P., and Shearing, C. (2009) *Lengthening the Arm of the Law Enhancing Police Resources in the Twenty-First Century*, Cambridge, Cambridge University Press.

Barker-Benfield, G. (1989) 'Mary Wollstonecraft: Eighteenth-Century Commonwealthwoman'. *Journal of the History of Ideas* 50(1): 95–115.

Barnes, T.D., Beaulieu, E., and Saxton G.W., (2017) 'Restoring trust in the police: Why female officers reduce suspicions of corruption' (gregorywsaxton.com) *Governance* 1–19. www.gregorywsaxton.com/uploads/5/4/3/0/54300059/barnes_et_al-2017-governance.pdf. Accessed 20/02/2021.

Bashir, M. (2020) 'Wembley Park murders: PCs "took selfies next to sisters' dead bodies"', BBC News, June 26. www.bbc.com/news/uk-england-london-53198702. Accessed 19/03/21.

BBC (2020) 'Small axe "red, white and blue"'. Small Axe – BBC Film, November 29. BBC One – Small Axe, Series 1, Red, White and Blue, Red, White and Blue: Who Is Leroy Logan? www.bbc.co.uk/programmes/p0901dz2. Accessed 19/02/2021.

Bows, H. (2017) 'Researching sexual violence against older people: Reflecting on the use of Freedom of Information requests in a feminist study'. *Feminist Review* 115(1): 30–45. doi: 10.1057/s41305-017-0029-z.

British Association for Women in Policing (BAWP) (2014) The Gender Agenda 3. London. http://bawp.org. Accessed 21/02/2015.

British Association for Women in Policing (BAWP) (2019) 'Heforshe – UK Policing Gender Equality Summit'. November 21. www.bawp.org/news/heforshe-uk-policing-gender-equality-summit/. Accessed 02/03/2020.

Brown, J. (2000) 'Discriminatory experiences of women police: A comparison of officers serving in England and Wales, Scotland, Northern Ireland and the Republic of Ireland'. *International Journal of the Sociology of Law* 28:(2) 91–111.

Brown, J., and Heidensohn, F. (2000) *Gender and Policing Comparative Perspectives*, Basingstoke, Palgrave Macmillan.

Brown, J., and King, J. (1998) 'Gender differences in police officers attitudes towards rape: Results of an exploratory study.' *Psychology, Crime & Law* 4(4): 265–79. doi: 10.1080/10683169808401760.

Brown, J., and Silvestri, M. (2019) 'A police service in transformation: Implications for women police officers'. *Police Practice and Research* 21(5): 459–475. doi: 10.1080/15614263.2019.1611206.

Brown, J., and Silvestri, M. (2020) 'Women policing in the United Kingdom: Transforming leadership', pp. 85–109. In (Ed) Rabe-Hemp, C., and Garcia, V. *Women Policing across the Globe*, London, Rowman and Littlefield.

Bryson, V. (1992) *Feminist Political Theory*, Hampshire, Macmillan.

Bucci, N. (2020) 'Victoria police officer dismissed for sexual harassment reinstated | Australian police and policing' | *The Guardian*, December 13. www.theguardian.com/australia-news/2020/dec/14/victoria-police-officer-dismissed-for-sexual-harassment-reinstated. Accessed 11/02/2021.

Busby, M. (2021) 'Fewer than one in 10 police officers fired after gross misconduct finding', *The Guardian*, January 18. www.theguardian.com/uk-news/2021/jan/18/fewer-than-one-in-10-police-officers-fired-after-gross-misconduct-finding. Accessed 11/02/2021.

Chadwick, P. (2018) 'From Peterloo to Ian Tomlinson: the Guardian's democratic duty', *The Guardian*, May 13. Accessed 22/02/2021.

Chakrabarti, S. (2021) 'After the Sarah Everard vigil scandal, who still thinks that the police need extra powers?' *The Guardian* Opinion, March 14. www.theguardian.com/commentisfree/2021/mar/14/sarah-everard-vigil-police-extra-powers-met-brutal-women-priti-patel-protestsAt: After the Sarah Everard vigil scandal, who still thinks the police need extra powers? Accessed 15/03/2021.

Chávez, K., Nair, Y., and Conrad, R. (2015) 'Equality, sameness, difference: Revisiting the Equal Rights Amendment'. *Women's Studies Quarterly* 43(3/4): 272–6 At: www.jstor.org/stable/43958573 Accessed 11/02/2021.

Condorcet, Marie-Jean Caritat, Marquis de (1790) 'On Giving Women the Right of Citizenship'. In McLean, I. and Hewitt, F. (1994) *Condorcet: Foundations of Social Choice and Political Theory*, Cheltenham, Edward Elgar.

Coole, D. (Ed) (1993) *Women in Political Theory* 2nd edition, Hertfordshire, Harvester Wheatsheaf.

Coote, A. and Pattulo, P. (1990) *Power and Prejudice: Women and Politics*, London, Weidenfeld & Nicolson.

Cordner G., and Cordner A. (2011) 'Stuck on a plateau? Obstacles to recruitment, selection and retention of women police'. *Police Quarterly* 14(3): 207–26. DOI:10.1177/1098611111413990

Crenshaw, K. (1989) 'Demarginalizing the intersection of race and sex: A Black feminist critique of antidiscrimination doctrine, feminist theory and

96 Bibliography

antiracist politics'. University of Chicago Legal Forum, 1989(1): article 8. https://chicagounbound.uchicago.edu/cgi/viewcontent.cgi?article=1052& context=uclf. Accessed 05/03/2021.

Crenshaw, K. (2017) Kimberlé Crenshaw on intersectionality, more than two decades later, Columbia Law School. www.law.columbia.edu/news/archive/kimberle-crenshaw-intersectionality-more-two-decades-later. Accessed 05/03/2021.

Cunningham, E., and Ramshaw, P. (2020) 'Twenty-three women officers' experiences of policing in England: The same old story or a different story?' *International Journal of Police Science and Management* 22(1): 26–37.

Day, E. (2019) '#BlackLivesMatter: the birth of a new civil rights movement', *The Guardian*, July 19. www.theguardian.com/world/2015/jul/19/blacklivesmatter-birth-civil-rights-movement. Accessed 03/03/2021.

De Gouges (1791) Ed. and Translated by Levy, D.G., Applewhite, H.B. and Johnson, M.D. (1980) *Women in Revolutionary Paris 1789–1795*, Champaign, University of Illinois Press.

Dick, G.P.M., and Metcalf, B. (2007) 'The progress of female police officers? An empirical analysis of organisational commitment and tenure explanations in two UK police forces'. *International Journal of Public Sector Management* 20(2): 81–100.

Dodd, V. (2018) 'Met police launch drive to balance the gender ranks', *The Guardian*, November 22. www.theguardian.com/uk-news/2018/nov/22/met-police-launches-drive-to-recruit-women-to-male-dominated-ranks. Accessed 11/02/2021.

Dodd, V. (2020) 'Watchdog investigates Met officers over Bianca Williams' treatment' *The Guardian*, October 8. www.theguardian.com/uk-news/2020/oct/08/met-police-to-investigate-officers-over-bianca-williams-treatment. Accessed 09/03/2021

Dodd, V. (2021) 'Met officer is taken off Sarah Everard duties over "offensive" WhatsApp image', *The Guardian*, March 15. www.theguardian.com/uk-news/2021/mar/15/sarah-everard-met-officer-removed-from-duties-for-sending-offensive-message. Accessed 19/03/2021.

Dodd, V., and Busby, M. (2020) 'Former top black Met police officers say racism blighted their careers'. *The Guardian*, June 15. www.theguardian.com/uk-news/2020/jun/14/former-top-met-police-officers-say-racism-blighted-their-careers-black. Accessed 11/02/2021.

Elgot, J. (2021) 'Domestic abuse bill: what amendments are peers voting on?' *The Guardian*, March 15. www.theguardian.com/society/2021/mar/15/domestic-abuse-bill-what-amendments-peers-voting-on. Accessed 19/03/2021.

Elshtain, J.B. (1981) *Public Man Private Woman: Women in Social and Political Thought*, Princeton, Princeton University Press.

Equality Act (2010) Legislation.gov.uk. At: www.legislation.gov.uk/ukpga/2010/15/contents. Accessed 19/02/2021.

Equality and Human Rights Commission. www.equalityhumanrights.com/sites/default/files/employercode.pdf.

Bibliography 97

Ferguson, M. (1992) *Routledge Revivals: Subject to Others, British Women Writers and Colonial Slavery*, 1670–1834 Oxon, Routledge. DOI:https://doi.org/10.4324/9781315758008

Green, K. (1995) *The Woman of Reason: Feminism, Humanism and Political Thought*, Oxford, Polity Press.

Gregory, J., and Lees, S. (1999) *Policing Sexual Assault*, London, Routledge.

Gorman, A. (2021) ' "Enough is enough!" Where, when and why March4Justice protests are taking place across Australia. *The Guardian*, March 14. www.theguardian.com/australia-news/2021/mar/15/march-4-justice-where-when-womens-march-protests-australia-march4justice-sydney-melbourne-canberra-brisbane. Accessed 14/03/2021.

The Guardian (2021) The Guardian view on violence against women: without safety, there can be no equality. *The Guardian*, March 11. www.theguardian.com/commentisfree/2021/mar/11/the-guardian-view-on-violence-against-women-without-safety-there-can-be-no-equality. Accessed 20/03/2021

Gunther Canada, W. (2001) *Rebel Writer: Mary Wollstonecraft and Enlightenment Politics*, DeKalb, Northern Illinois University Press.

Harding, S. (1987) Ed, *Feminism and Methodology*, Indianapolis and Bloomington. Indiana University Press.

Harding, S. (1991) *Whose Science? Whose Knowledge?* Ithaca, N.Y, Cornell University Press | 2016 https://doi.org/10.7591/9781501712951.

Heidensohn, F. (2002) 'Gender and crime'. In Maguire M., Morgan R., and Reiner R. (Eds.) *The Oxford Handbook of Criminology*, Oxford, Oxford University Press, 491–530.

Heidensohn, F. (2009) 'Models of justice: Portia or Persephone? Some thoughts on equality, fairness and gender in the field of criminal justice'. In Newburn, T. (Ed) *Key Readings in Criminology*. Cullompton, Willan, 287–98 [Original published 1986].

Heidensohn, F. (2012) 'The future of feminist criminology'. *Crime, Media Culture: An International Journal* 8(2): 123–34. https://doi.org/10.1177/1741659012444431

Henley, J. (2009) 'A force to be reckoned with', *The Guardian*, August 21. www.theguardian.com/politics/2009/aug/22/women-police-officers-climate-camp. Accessed 30/08/2009.

Home Office (2004) *Initial Police Learning and Development Programme. Guidance for Chief Officers and Police Authorities*, London, Home Office.

hooks, b (2000) *Feminism Is for Everybody: Passionate Politics*, Cambridge, MA, Southend Press.

Hunt Botting, E., and Carey, C. (2004) 'Wollstonecraft's Philosophical Impact on Nineteenth-Century American Women's Rights Advocates'. *American Journal of Political Science* 48: 4(Oct): 707–722.

Independent Office for Police Conduct (IOPC) (2020) 'Recommendation – Greater Manchester Police', December 2020, Independent Office for Police Conduct. www.policeconduct.gov.uk/recommendations/recommendation-greater-manchester-police-december-2020. Accessed 11/02/2021.

98   *Bibliography*

Independent Police Complaints Commission (IPCC) (2011) *Corruption in the Police Service in England and Wales.* https://assets.publishing.service.gov.uk/government/uploads/system/uploads/attachment_data/file/229007/9780108510991.pdf. Accessed 11/02/2021.

Irving, R. (2009) 'Career trajectories of women in policing in Australia', Australian Institute of Criminology. Trends and issues in Crime and Criminal justice 37, 1–6. www.aic.gov.au/publications/tandi/tandi370. Accessed 19/02/2021.

Jackson, L.A. (2006) *Women Police: Gender, Welfare and Surveillance in the Twentieth Century*, Manchester and New York, Manchester University Press.

Jones, M., and Rowe, M. (2015) 'Sixteen years on: Examining the role of diversity within contemporary policing'. *Policing a Journal of Policy and Practice* 9(1): 2–4.

Jones, S. (1986) *Policewomen and Equality*, London, Macmillan Press Limited.

Kelly, J. (2021) 'Coronavirus: Domestic abuse an "epidemic beneath a pandemic"', BBC News, www.bbc.com/news/uk-56491643, March 23. Accessed 23/03/2021.

Kennedy, E., and Mendus, S. Eds. (1987) *Women in Western Political Philosophy: Kant to Nietzsche*, Brighton, Wheatsheaf.

King, P. (1983) *The History of Ideas:An introduction to method*, London and Canberra, Croom Helm.

Kitts, S.A. (1994) 'Mary Wollstonecraft's a vindication of the rights of woman: A judicious response from eighteenth century Spain'. *The Modern Language Review* 89(2): 351–9.

Lather, P. (1988) 'Feminist perspectives on empowering research methodologies'. *Women's Studies International Forum* 11(6): 569–81.

Laverick, W. (2021) Women in policing. In Joyce, P., and Laverick, W. (Eds.) 2nd edition, *Policing: Development and Contemporary Practice*, Newbury Park, London, CA, SAGE, 177–205.

Laverick, W., and Cain, L. (2015) 'The gender agenda in an age of austerity'. *Policing* 9(4): 362–76.

Laverick, W., Joyce, P., Calvey, D., and Cain, L. (2019) 'The menopause and the female workforce'. *British Journal of Community Justice* 15(2): 59–81.

Lewis, P. (2011) 'Tottenham riots: a peaceful protest, then suddenly all hell broke loose', *The Guardian*, August 7. www.theguardian.com/uk/2011/aug/07/tottenham-riots-peaceful-protest. Accessed 11/02/2021.

Lister, R. (1997) *Citizenship Feminist Perspectives*, Hampshire, Macmillan.

Loftus, B. (2008) 'Dominant culture interrupted: Recognition, Resentment and the politics of change in an English Police force'. *British Journal of Criminology* 48(6): 778–97.

Machiavelli, N. (First written 1513 – first published 1532/1974) *The Prince,* Translated with an introduction by George Bull, London, Penguin.

Machiavelli, N. (1518 – published 1531/1970) *The Discourses on the First Ten Books of Titus Livius* (Ed) Bernard Crick. Translated by Leslie J. Walker, S.J. Revisions by Brian Richardson London, Penguin.

Bibliography 99

Martin, C. (1996) 'The impact of equal opportunities policies on the day-to-day experiences of women police constables'. *British Journal of Criminology* 36(4): 510–28.

Martin, S.E. (1980) *Breaking and Entering. Policewomen on Patrol*, London, University of California Press.

Maryonthegreen (2020) www.maryonthegreen.org. Accessed 19/03/2020.

McRobbie, A. (1982) 'The politics of feminist research: Between talk, text and action'. *Feminist Review* 12(Oct): 46–57.

Millen, D. (1997) 'Some methodological and epistemological issues raised by doing feminist research on non-feminist women'. *Sociological Research Online* 2(3): 114–28 ww.socresonline.org.uk/socresonline/2/3/3.html. Accessed 23/09/1998.

Moller-Okin, S. (1979) *Women in Western Political Thought*, Princeton, Princeton University Press.

Muir, H. (2021) 'Black and blue: the secret lives of BAME police officers' | Police | *The Guardian*, February 7. www.theguardian.com/uk-news/2021/feb/07/black-and-blue-the-secret-lives-of-bame-police-officers. Accessed 16/02/2021.

Newman, C. (2021) 'Former top Met Police officer Nusrit Mehtab sues over "racial and sexist abuse"', Channel 4 News, February 11, www.channel4.com/news/former-top-met-police-officer-nusrit-mehtab-sues-over-racial-and-sexist-abuse. Accessed 12/02/21.

Newsround, BBC (2019) '100 Years of Women in the Met Police'. CBBC Newsround, February 15. www.bbc.co.uk/newsround/47254533. Accessed 09/02/2021.

Novak, K.J., Brown, R.A., and Frank, J. (2011) 'Women on patrol: an analysis of differences in officer arrest behaviour'. *Policing: An International Journal* 34(4): 566–87. doi: 10.1108/13639511111180216.

Offen, K. (2000) *European Feminisms 1700–1900: A Political History*, Stanford, Stanford University Press.

Parliament TV (2021) 'Jess Phillips reads out names of women killed in Britain in the last year', video. *The Guardian*, March 11. www.theguardian.com/politics/video/2021/mar/11/jess-phillips-reads-out-names-of-women-killed-in-britain-in-the-last-year-video.

Pateman, C. (1988) 'The patriarchal welfare state'. In Gutmann, A. (Ed.) *Democracy and the Welfare State*, Princeton, Princeton University Press, 194–233.

Pateman, C. (1995) 'Equality, difference, subordination: the politics of motherhood and women's citizenship'. In Bock, G., and James, S. (Eds.) *Beyond Equality and Difference*, London and New York, Routledge, 17–31.

Perkin, J. (2002) *Women and Marriage in Nineteenth-Century England*, London, Routledge.

Police Workforce (2020) 'Police workforce, England and Wales: 31 March 2020 third edition'. www.gov.uk/government/statistics/police-workforce-england-and-wales-31-march-2020. Accessed 06/05/2020.

Rabe-Hemp, C.E. (2008a). 'Female officers and the ethic of care: Does officer gender impact police behaviors?' *Journal of Criminal Justice* 36: 426–34. doi: 10.1016/j.jcrimjus.2008.07.001.

100 Bibliography

Rabe-Hemp, C.E. (2008b). 'Survival in an "all-boys club": Policewomen and their fight for acceptance'. *Policing: An International Journal of Police Strategies & Management* 31: 251–70. doi.10.1108/13639510810878712

Reiner, R. (1992) 'Policing a postmodern society'. *The Modern Law Review* 55(6): 761–81.

Renzetti C.M. (2013) *Feminist Criminology*, London, Routledge.

Roman, I. (2020) 'Women in policing: the numbers fall far short of the need'. *Police Chief Magazine*, April 22. www.policechiefmagazine.org/women-in-policing. Accessed 16/02/21.

Rousseau, J.J. (1762/1972) *Emile*, London, Everyman Dent. Translated by Foxley, B.

Rousseau, J.J. (1762/1968) *The Social Contract* with introduction by Cranston, M. (1968), London, Penguin.

Rowlatt, B. (2016) *In Search of Mary: The Mother of All Journeys*, London, Alma.

Rowlatt, B. (2019) 'An Amazon Stept Out', directed by Honor Borwick with musical contributions assembled by Harriet Houghton Slade Sept 30, Lyric Theatre London. https://wearethecity.com/30-09-19-an-amazon-stept-out-wollstonecraft-society/

Russell, B. (1961) *A History of Western Philosophy*, London, Allen and Unwin.

Sapiro, V. (1992) *A Vindication of Political Virtue: The Political Theory of Mary Wollstonecraft*, Chicago, University of Chicago Press.

Scarman, L.G. (1981) The Brixton Disorders 10–12 April 1981. The Scarman Report. London, Penguin.

Scott, J.W. (1988) 'Deconstructing equality-versus-difference: or, the uses of poststructuralist theory for feminism'. *Feminist Studies* 14(1)(Spring): 32–50. doi: 10.1017/CBO9780511570940.020

Siddique, H. (2021) 'Civil liberties groups call police plans for demos an "assault" on right to protest'. *The Guardian*, March 11. www.theguardian.com/law/2021/mar/11/civil-liberties-groups-call-police-plans-for-demos-an-assault-on-right-to-protest. Accessed 15/03/2021.

Silvestri, M. (2017) 'Police culture and gender: revisiting the 'cult of masculinity'. *Policing* 11(3): 289–300. doi: 10.1093/police/paw052.

Silvestri, M. (2018) 'Disrupting the "heroic" male within policing: A case of direct entry'. *Feminist Criminology* 13(3): 309–28. doi:10.1177/1557085118763737

Simpson, R., and Croft, A. (2020) 'Seeing gender in policing: Uniforms and perceived aggression'. *Women & Criminal Justice*. doi: 10.1080/08974454.2020.1842290.

Skolnick, J.H. (2008) 'Enduring issues of police culture and demographics'. *Policing and Society: An International Journal of Research and Policy* 18(1). doi: 10.1080/10439460701718542.

Squires, J. (2000) *Gender in Political Theory*, Cambridge, Polity Press.

Squires, J. (2003) 'Equality and Diversity: A New Equality Framework for Britain?' At: www.swern.co.uk/esml/Library/pdf-files/squires.pdf. Accessed 20/01/2020.

Squires, J. (2007) *The New Politics of Gender Equality*, Basingstoke, Palgrave Macmillan.

Bibliography   101

Stinson, P.M., Todak, N.E., and Dodge, M. (2014) 'An exploration of crime by policewomen'. *Police Practice and Research*, 16(1): 79–93. doi: 10.1080/15614263.2013.846222.

Taylor, B. (1983) *Eve and the New Jerusalem*, London, Virago.

Thorpe, V. (2020) '"I need complete freedom": Maggi Hambling responds to statue critics', *The Guardian*, November 14. www.theguardian.com/artanddesign/2020/nov/14/i-need-complete-freedom-maggi-hambling-responds-to-statue-critics. Accessed 20/01/2021.

Tomalin, C. (1992) *The Life and Death of Mary Wollstonecraft* 2nd edition, London, Penguin.

Townsend, M. (2012) 'Senior officer calls for watchdog after Met police racism revelations', *The Guardian*, April 7. www.theguardian.com/uk/2012/apr/07/racism-metropolitan-police-stephen-lawrence. Accessed 21/03/2021.

Townsend, M., and Jayanetti, C. 2021 'Revealed: the grim list of sex abuse claims against Metropolitan police'. *The Guardian*, March 20. www.theguardian.com/uk-news/2021/mar/20/revealed-the-grim-list-of-sex-abuse-claims-against-metropolitan-police. Accessed 21/03/2021.

VEOHRC (2019) 'Independent review into sex discrimination and sexual harassment, including predatory behaviour, in Victoria Police: Phase 3 audit and review'. Victorian Equal Opportunity & Human Rights Commission (VEOHRC), Carlton, Victoria 3053, Australia. www.humanrights.vic.gov.au/legal-and-policy/research-reviews-and-investigations/police-review/. Accessed 10/01/2020.

Waugh, L., Ede, A., and Alley, A. (1998) 'Police culture, women police and attitudes towards misconduct'. *International Journal of Police Science & Management* 1(3): 288–300. doi: 10.1177/146135579800100307

Westmarland, L. (2001) *Gender and Policing: Sex Power and Police Culture*, Cullompton, Willan.

Westmarland, L., and Rowe, M. (2018) 'Police ethics and integrity, can a new code overturn the blue code?' *Policing and Society: An International Journal of Research and Policy* 28(7): 854–70. doi: 10.1080/10439463.2016.1262365.

Wilkinson, V., and Froyland, I.D. (1996) 'Women in policing'. Australian Government, Australian Institute of Criminology. *Trends and Issues in Crime and Criminal Justice* no. 58: 1–6. www.aic.gov.au/publications/tandi/tandi58.

Wollstonecraft, M. (1787/1989) 'Thoughts on the education of daughters: With reflections on female conduct, in the more important duties of life'. In *The Works of Mary Wollstonecraft*, volume 4, (Eds.) Todd, J., and Butler, M., London, Routledge.

Wollstonecraft, M. (1790/1994) 'A vindication of the rights of men, in a letter to the Right Honourable Edmund Burke'. In *Mary Wollstonecraft*, Political Writings: A Vindication of the Rights of Men, A Vindication of the Rights of Woman and An Historical and Moral View of the French Revolution. Ed Todd, J. Oxford, Oxford University Press.

102 *Bibliography*

Wollstonecraft, M. (1792/1992) *A Vindication of the Rights of Woman with Strictures on Moral and Political Subjects* (Ed) Miriam Brody, London, Penguin.

Wollstonecraft, M. (1796/ 1987) 'Letters written during a short residence in Sweden, Norway and Denmark'. In *A Short Residence in Sweden and Memoirs of the Author of the Rights of Woman* (Ed) Holmes, R. London, Penguin.

Woodeson, A. (1993) 'The first women police: a force for equality or infringement?' *Women's History Review* 2(2): 217–32. doi: 10.1080/0961 2029300200025.

Yoder J.D. (1991) 'Rethinking tokenism: looking beyond numbers'. *Gender and Society* 5(2): 178–92.

Index

Note: Tables in this index are shown in **bold** type. Entries including "force" relate to the use of coercion whereas entries including "Force" relate to the police service.

abuse of authority **57**, 57, **58**, **59**, **62**, **65–7**, 69, 70, 80, 88
abuse of power 43, 73, 77, 88, 89, 90
accountability 42, 43, 51, 79
aggression 37, 40, 51, 52, 53, 56, 74, 81, 88
arrest behaviours 51
attitudes: racist 7; sexist 4, 41; to women 11, 44, 48; to women police officers 33, 34, 36–7, 43, 50–1
Australia, policing in 27–48, 87, 88, 90–1; and feminist use of Freedom of Information requests 51, 52, 54, 74, 78, 80, 81, 82, 84
authority 20, 89; abuse of **57**, 57, **58**, **59**, **62**, **65–7**, 69, 70, 80, 88
authority, respect, and courtesy breaches **60**, **61**, **62**, 62, 63, **64**, 65, **66**, **68**, **69**, 70
autonomy 21–2

BAME (Black, Asian and Minority Ethnic) population: communities 40, 55–6; officers 4, 5–6, 6–7, 29, 32, 34, 38–9; *see also* minorities
'banter' 29, 31, 55, 56
behaviours: aggressive 37, 40, 51, 52, 53, 56, 74, 81, 88; arrest 51; controlling 50; disciplinary 81; ethical 25, 39–40; gendered 4, 23, 25–6, 51, 54, 55, 89, 90;

misogynistic 82–3; police officer 49, 54, 55, 56, 80–1; racist 29; risk averse 50, 79; sexist 47; sexual role 25
biases 7, 29, 43, 45
blocked opportunities 36, 54, 56
brutality, police 5, 50
Burke, Edmund 13, 15, 16, 17–18, 19, 22

care responsibilities 32, 38, 42
cautions **59**, **65**, **67**
challenging and reporting improper conduct breaches **64**, 65
childbearing 21, 37, 92
childcare 23, 32, 34, 37, 88
citizenship 1, 9, 10, 11, 16, 45, 92
communication skills 29, 53
community policing 39, 53, 88, 91
community reassurance 36
confidentiality breaches **57**, 57, **58**, **59**, **60**, **61**, **62**, 62, 63, **64**, 64, 65, **72**, **74**, **75**, 75
consent, policing by 49, 54
Constabulary Police area **65–9**, 69–70, **71**, 78
controlling behaviours 50
corruption 21, 49–50, 79, 92
criminal convictions **65**, **67**, 70
criminal networks 50, 79
criminal offences **57**, 57, **58**, **59**

104 *Index*

criminology 2, 4, 10, 41
culture *see* policing culture

dangerous assignments 53
dangerousness, of women 15, 16, 19–23
data collection 52, 54–5, 80
death in custody **73**, 73, **77**, 77, 79, 80, 88
derogatory remarks, about women 9, 29, 30
Dick, Commissioner Cressida 7, 39, 52, 83, 84, 92
difference and sameness debate 1–7, 10, 31, 48, 86
difference dilemma 15, 26, 36
disciplinary action 56, **56**, **66**, 78
disciplinary behaviours 81
disciplinary breaches 51
disciplinary data 49, 51, 81, 83, 88, 92
disciplinary offences 4, 25, 26, 88, 91; and feminist use of Freedom of Information requests 51, 52, 53, 54, 73, 79, 80
disciplinary problems 32
disciplinary proceedings 55, **66**
disciplinary records 2, 4, 6, 52, 53, 54, 78–9, 81, 85, 92–3
discourse analysis 10
Discourse on the Origin of Inequality, A 19–20
discreditable conduct **60**, **61**, 62–3, **64**, 65, **65–9**, 70, **71**
discrimination 6, 9, 46–7; gendered 82; racial 5; sex *see* sex discrimination; structural 37
dishonesty **73**, 74, **77**, 78
dismissal 7, 47–8, **58**, **59**, **60**, **61**, **65–6**, **68–9**
diversity 26, 38, 44–5, 46, **60**, **61**, **62**, 63, **64**, 65, **72**, 75, **76**
divine rights 17, 20
drink driving **71**, **74**, **75**, 75
duties, of women 21, 23
duties and responsibilities breaches **60**, **61**, 62–3, **64**, 64–5, **65–6**, **67–9**, 70, **71**

education, of women 17, 21, 92
Emile 20–1

Enquiry Concerning the Origin of Our Ideas of the Sublime and the Beautiful 17–18
epistemology 3, 13
Equal Opportunity and Human Rights Commission 27, 42, 44, 51
equal rights, for men and women 23, 24, 45
Equal Rights Amendment (ERA) 45
equality, gender 5, 6, 39, 42, 43–4
equality and diversity breaches **60**, **61**, **62**, 63, **64**, 65, **72**, 75, **76**
ERA (Equal Rights Amendment) 45
ethics 3, 4, 12–13, 25, 38, 39–40, 50, 51, 55, 78, 80–1, 89
Everard, Sarah 81–2, 82–3, 84, 92, 93

failure in duty breaches **65**, **67**, 70, **71**
fairness 29, 53, 89
fast track action **56**
female representation, in policing 33, 34, 39, 53, 57, 84, 87, 91
feminine moral superiority 25, 74
femininity 24, 40, 50–1
feminism 8, 10, 11, 12–13, 13–14, 24, 42–3, 83, 87
feminist intersectional critique 85
feminist theory 8, 28, 44–5
final written warning **68–9**, **71**
fines **66**
fitness for duty breaches **60**, **61**, **62**, **64**
FOI requests *see* Freedom of Information (FOI) requests
force 25–6, 35, 51–2, 53, 55; *see also* force/abuse of authority; use of force
Force Police area **71–3**, 73–4, **74–5**, 75, **76–7**, 77, **78**, 78, 80
force/abuse of authority **57**, 57, **58**, **59**, **60**; *see also* force; use of force
formal action 56, **56**, **60**, **61**, **62**, 63–5, **64**
formal discipline **56**
formal misconduct **56**, **58**, **59**
Freedom of Information (FOI) requests 4, 49–85, **56**, **57**, **58–62**, **64**, **65–9**, **71–3**, **74–5**, **76–7**, **78**

gender bias 45
gender equality 5, 6, 39, 42, 43–4

Index 105

gender hierarchy 13
gender norms 8
gender representation 33, 34, 39, 53, 57, 78, 84, 87, 91
gender stereotypes 50
gender wage gap 2, 32, 42
gendered behaviours 4, 23, 25–6, 51, 54, 55, 89, 90
gendered discrimination 82
general conduct breaches **57**, 57, **58**, **59**, **62**, **65–6**, **66–8**, 69, 70
gross misconduct 82

harassment 28, 36, 42, **72**, 74–5, **74**, **75**, 80, 82, 84, 87; sexual 2, 4, 25, 33, 41, 42, 47, 54, 56, **72**, 74–5, **74**, **75**, 81
high-stress assignments 53
honesty and integrity breaches **57**, 57, **58**, **59**, **60**, **61**, **62**, 62, 63, **64**, **66**, **69**, 70
human rights 1, 5, 10, 13, 83, 87, 89, 92; and the nature of woman 41, 43, 46
Human Rights Commission 27, 42, 44, 51
hypermasculinity 12, 13, 25, 40, 41, 43

ideal male officer 10, 30–1, 87
identification parade irregularities 73, 77, **78**, 78
identity 16, 32–3, 41, 48, 86
impartiality 44, 46, 54
inappropriate association **72**, **74**, **75**, 75
inappropriate relationships with victims of crime **72**, 73, 75, **76**, **77**, 77, 80, 88
incivility **72**, 75, 76
inclusion, of women in policing 2, 19, 25, 26, 28, 46, 51, 54; *see also* integration, of women in policing
Independent Office for Police Conduct (IOPC) 52, 55, 82
Initial Police Learning and Development Programme (IPLDP) 1
institutional misogyny 83
institutional racism 7, 39, 83

Integrated Rainbow Information System (IRIS), misuse of **71**, **74**, **75**, 75, **76**, **77**, 77
integration, of women in policing 2, 10, 23–6, 27–8, 43–4, 49; *see also* inclusion, of women in policing
intersectionality 91
IOPC (Independent Office for Police Conduct) 52, 55, 82
IPLDP (Initial Police Learning and Development Programme) 1
IRIS (Integrated Rainbow Information System), misuse of **71**, **74**, **75**, 75, **76**, **77**, 77

law enforcement 32, 36
leadership 5, 7, 43, 83
legitimacy, of policing 2, 4, 25, 39, 40, 88, 90, 91, 92; and feminist use of Freedom of Information requests 49, 50, 51, 53, 82, 83, 84, 85
limitations, of Freedom of Information research methodology 54–6
Locke, John 17, 18

mainstreaming 45, 46
male ideal, of the police officer 29, 42, 86–7
male model, of policing 40
male privilege 43, 48, 79, 89
male representation, in policing 78
male supremacy 18–19
male violence 82, 83, 84
male-dominated professions 8, 9
management action 56, **56**, 63, **71**
management advice 57, **60**, **61**, **64**, **65–6**, **68–9**, **71**
masculinity 23, 40, 41, 43, 54, 84; hyper- 12, 13, 25, 40, 41, 43; toxic 29, 54, 81, 91
methodology, research 3, 4, 12, 14, 53–4
methods, research 12, 51, 53, 54, 88
Metropolitan Police Service (MPS) 5, 7, 38, 82, 83, 85, 92
minorities 34, 39, 45–6; *see also* BAME (Black, Asian and Minority Ethnic) population
misconceptions, about women 16, 26

106 *Index*

misconduct 7, 51, 52, 55, **62**, **72**, 82, 85, 88; formal **56**, **58**, **59**; gross 82; hearings for **67**; in public office **72**, 75, **76**; meetings for **67**–9
misogyny 4, 29, 31, 48, 86, 88, 89, 90, 91, 92–3; and feminist use of Freedom of Information requests 52, 54, 79, 81, 82–3, 84–5; institutional 83
misuse of force 80
misuse of force electronic and communication policy 70
misuse of IRIS (Integrated Rainbow Information System) **71**, **74**, **75**, 75, **76**, **77**, 77
misuse of Police National Computer (PNC) **65**, **67**, 70, **78**, 78
modern feminism 10, 11
'modern' woman officer 33
moral superiority 25, 74
motherhood 9, 20
MPS (Metropolitan Police Service) 5, 7, 38, 82, 83, 85, 92

nature of woman 8–26, 27–48, 86–7, 88, 89, 91–2; and feminist use of Freedom of Information requests 49, 51, 52–3, 79, 81, 84
neighbourhood policing 39, 53, 88, 91
not following lawful orders **57**, **58**

offences: criminal **57**, 57, **58**, **59**; disciplinary *see* disciplinary offences; profit-related 52, 80, 81; sexual **72**, 74, **74**, **75**, 80, 81; violence-related 81
officers in uniform 51, 52, 81
orders and instructions breaches **60**, **61**, 62, 63, **64**, 65, **66**, **68**, 70
outsider status 50, 79, 88, 89

Pateman, Carole 15, 16, 19, 26, 36, 44–8
patriarchy 3, 8, 12, 13, 17, 21, 43, 79, 81, 84, 88, 89, 90, 92
patrol officers 37
pay gap 2, 6, 32, 34, 42, 88
pension inequalities 6, 32, 34, 42, 88
'people skills' 35, 36

PEQF (Policing Education Qualifications Framework) 1
performance of duties breaches **57**, 57, **58**, **59**, **65**, **66**–8, 69, 70
PNC (Police National Computer), misuse of **65**, **67**, 70, **78**, 78
police accountability 42, 43, 51, 79
police brutality 5, 50
police disciplinary records 85, 92–3
police ethics 55, 78
Police National Computer (PNC), misuse of **65**, **67**, 70, **78**, 78
police officer behaviours 49, 54, 55, 56, 80–1
police recruitment 1, 6, 7, 33, 34, 39, 87
police vehicle accident **73**, 74, **76**, **77**, 77
police-citizen encounters 4, 25–6, 39, 51–2
policewomen *see* women police officers
policing: in Australia *see* Australia, policing in; community 39, 53, 88, 91; by consent 49, 54; inclusion of women into 2, 19, 25, 26, 28, 46, 51, 54; integration of women into 2, 10, 23–6, 27–8, 43–4, 49; legitimacy of *see* legitimacy, of policing; neighbourhood 39, 53, 88, 91; public order 25, 33, 40, 83, 84, 91
policing behaviours 49, 54, 55, 56, 80–1
policing culture 1, 2–3, 4, 87, 88, 90, 91; and feminist use of Freedom of Information requests 49, 51, 52, 54, 56, 81, 82–3; and the nature of woman 12, 13, 14, 28, 32, 33, 36, 41, 43, 47
Policing Education Qualifications Framework (PEQF) 1
policing legitimacy *see* legitimacy, of policing
policing literature 3, 16, 28, 32, 86
policing policy 6, 27, 49–50
policing practice 13, 55–6
policing styles 5, 25; of women police officers 39, 40, 43, 50, 79, 84, 86, 88, 89

Index 107

policing tactics 33, 40, 83
policy: policing 6, 27, 49–50; societal
    11, 38, 45, 84
politeness and tolerance breaches **57**,
    57, **58**, **59**, **65**, **67–8**, 70
political theory 15, 22
power 9, 20, 22, 48, 84, 88, 89, 90, 91,
    92; abuse of 43, 73, 77, 88, 89, 90
practice, police 13, 55–6
presences 33
profit-related offences 52, 80, 81
promotion 1, 7, 38, 42
proto-feminism 10
public order policing 25, 33, 40, 83,
    84, 91

racial discrimination 5
racial profiling 55–6
racially motivated violence 5, 50
racism 4, 5–6, 7, 29, 46–7, 84–5, 92;
    institutional 7, 39, 83
rank reduction **65**, **67**
recruitment 1, 6, 7, 33, 34, 39, 87
reduced in rank **65**, **67**
regulations, breaches of 62, 63, 79
representation, in policing 29, 53;
    BAME 5, 6, 32, 34, 38–9; of men
    78; of women 33, 34, 39, 53, 57, 84,
    87, 91
reprimands **58**, **59**, **65**, **66**, **67**
research methodology 3, 4, 12, 14,
    53–4
research methods 12, 51, 53, 54, 88
retention 6, 7, 23, 39, 87
Review of Policing 28, 34, 41, 42
review of policing, in Australia 42–4,
    54
rights: divine 17, 20; equal 23, 24,
    45; human *see* human rights;
    vindication of 3, 16–17, 19
risk aversion 50, 79, 88, 89
Rousseau, Jean-Jacques vii, 13, 15,
    16, 17, 19–22, 23, 24

sameness and difference debate 1–7,
    10, 31, 48, 86
sameness and difference dilemma
    15–17, 27, 45
Scott, Joan W. 10, 15–16, 19, 26, 36,
    42, 86

senior ranks 33, 38
Service police area 56–65, **56–62**, **64**
sex discrimination 2, 4, 25, 28, 29, 33,
    41, 42, 43, 47
sexism 4, 12, 13, 84, 87, 92; and the
    nature of woman 28, 31, 41, 46–7
sex-related offences **72**, 74, **74**, **75**,
    80, 81
sexual double standard 22, 23
sexual harassment 2, 4, 25, 33, 41, 42,
    47; and feminist use of Freedom
    of Information requests 54, 56, **72**,
    74–5, **74**, **75**, 81
sexual offences **72**, 74, **74**, **75**, 80, 81
sexual role behaviours 25
sexuality 4, 6, 12, 16, 30, 54–5, 92
sharing of an image 74, 77, 80
Social Contract, The 20
social maternalism 24, 31
socialization, of women 22
societal policy 11, 38, 45, 84
specialist expertise, of women police
    officers 24–5
Squires, Judith 27, 42, 44–5, 46, 86
stereotypes 4, 8, 25, 35, 50, 51, 57,
    74, 77
stop and search 54, 55, 83
structural discrimination 37
structural support 6, 87
subjection, of women 9
superintendent warnings **65**, **66–7**
surveillance, of women 22, 23

tactics, policing 33, 40, 83
*Thoughts on the Education of
    Daughters* 8–9
toxic masculinity 29, 54, 81, 91
traditional role, of women police
    officers 36
'traditional' woman police officer 33
transformative change, in policing
    practice 2, 6, 87, 89–90, 91, 92;
    and feminist use of Freedom of
    Information requests 27, 39, 41, 42,
    43–4, 45, 46, 48
transparency 54
trust, in the police 5, 25, 40, 87, 88,
    92; and feminist use of Freedom
    of Information requests 49–50, 51,
    52, 53, 54

108 *Index*

uniform: officers in 51, 52, 81; unsuitability of women's 29–30, 73, 78, 86–7
use of force 25, 55, 75, 81; breaches due to **57**, 57, **60**, **61**, **62**, 62, 63; *see also* force; force/abuse of authority

VAWG (Violence Against Women and Girls) 84
Victoria Police, Australia 2–3, 42, 47, 74, 78, 91
Vindication of the Rights of Men, A 3, 16, 19
Vindication of the Rights of Woman, A 3, 16–17, 19
Violence Against Women and Girls (VAWG) 84
violence-related offences 81

wage gap 2, 6, 32, 34, 42, 88
weakness, of women 8, 17–19, 32, 37
Wollstonecraft, Mary 3, 5, 8–26, 27, 43, 44, 46, 86, 92; dilemma of 15, 16, 19, 26, 36, 44–8

woman, nature of *see* nature of woman
woman as different arguments 16, 17–23, 30–1, 35, 36, 46, 52–3
women: attitudes towards 4, 7, 11, 33, 34, 36–7, 41, 43, 44, 48, 50–1; dangerousness of 15, 16, 19–23; as different *see* woman as different arguments; education of 17, 21, 92; exclusion from citizenship of 16; inclusion in policing of 2, 19, 25, 26, 28, 46, 51, 54; integration in policing of 2, 10, 23–6, 27–8, 43–4, 49; misconceptions about 26; nature of *see* nature of woman; socialization of 22; subjection of 9; surveillance of 22, 23; weakness of 8, 17–19, 32, 37
women police officers: derogatory remarks about 9, 29, 30; duties of 21, 23; specialist expertise of 24–5
workplace harms 41, 42, 43, 44
written warnings **56**, **60**, **61**, **64**, **65–6**, **67–8**, 79; final **68–9**, **71**

Milton Keynes UK
Ingram Content Group UK Ltd.
UKHW022225131124
451128UK00003B/8